More to Life Than Having It All

BOB WELCH

HARVEST HOUSE PUBLISHERS
Eugene, Oregon 97402

Cover illustration © 1991 David Slonim

MORE TO LIFE THAN HAVING IT ALL

Copyright © 1992 by Harvest House Publishers
Eugene, Oregon 97402

Library of Congress Cataloging-in-Publication Data

Welch, Bob, 1954- .
    More to life than having it all / Bob Welch.
    Includes bibliographical references.
    ISBN 0-89081-892-4
    1. Values.   2. Christian life—1960- .   3. Baby boom gener-
ation—Conduct of life.   I. Title.
BD431.W333   1992   91-14201
241—dc20   CIP

For the girl up the street,
Sally Jean.

With Appreciation To:

- My sons, Ryan and Jason Welch, for patience, understanding and rescheduling upstairs basketball games while I was doing downstairs writing.

- Pastor Rick Taylor, for encouraging me to risk.

- Eileen Mason of Harvest House, for allowing me to risk.

- Sandy Silverthorne, for listening patiently to my ideas—even the duds.

- Linda Crew, for the advice of a proven author and loyal sister.

- Robbin Stewart, for editing insight from 3,000 miles away.

- Michael Stewart, for pep talks, prayer and paying the hefty phone bills for much of Robbin's editing insight from 3,000 miles away.

C O N T E N T S

Understanding the Cultural Forces

Understanding the Cultural Forces

ε∂

A phone call interrupts the uncharacteristic quiet of the news room on this August morning. As a newspaper columnist, I am prepared to receive an array of eye-opening story ideas from readers—everything from the elderly man who is sure he's seen Bigfoot in a Sears parking lot to the woman who has had her deceased dog freeze-dried.

But I am not prepared for this caller. A man in his early 40s, he wonders if I am interested in writing a story about a 15-year-old boy, the son of two well-heeled, have-it-all professionals whose large suburban house features a Porsche and Mercedes in the garage.

"What's so interesting about this kid?" I ask.

"Well," says the man, "he's a cocaine dealer."

"And how do you know him?"

There is a pause on the other end of the line. "Because," the man says, "he is my son."

The man has called because he believes a newspaper article might help people realize what's happening across the country. "It's not just my son," he says. "It's lots of people's sons and lots of people's daughters who are deeply into drugs. We're not talking about ghetto kids. We're talking about typical American families."

The man isn't finished. "Last night my son tried to kill himself. Do you know what that's like for a father? Do you know what it's like to see your son—the same son you coached in Little League a few years ago—lying in a hospital emergency room after trying to commit suicide?"

From the streets of suburbia, in an affluent community where one might believe the biggest problem would be sidewalk skateboarders, the father's chilling question echoes the angst of America. Fortunately, only some people experience the pain as acutely as this father and son. Unfortunately, many are still struggling for some semblance of fulfillment.

The sky may not be falling, but ominous clouds are darkening the social horizon. "As a society," said Yale psychology professor Edward Zigler, "we're at a breaking point as far as family is concerned."[1]

Some retaliate with lame humor. "I've got a drug problem," read one bumper sticker a few years ago, "I'm all out." A TV game show now pokes fun at divorce as if it were the sociological equivalent of bumping one's crazy bone. A comedian jokes about the yuppie wife who goes into a frenzy after realizing she's left the mall with the wrong baby. "Shhh," says her husband, "it's a better stroller."

As we slide unsteadily toward a new century, however, nobody's laughing. A not-so-funny thing happened on the way to the self-fulfillment forum: Addictions, divorce and misplaced priorities have fractured families. Too many mothers are missing their children's childhoods. And instead of playing catch on the front lawn, too many fathers are meeting their sons in hospital emergency rooms.

In 1990, a national commission that included the American Medical Association released a report on today's teenagers, a report whose very name—"Code Blue"—suggested the seriousness of its findings. "Many of America's young people, both rich and poor, from all racial and ethnic backgrounds, have serious social, emotional and health problems, problems that have potentially disastrous consequences not only for the individual teen, but for society as a whole," it said. In the past, every generation of American teenagers has been healthier, better cared for and better prepared for life than their parents, said the report.

"This generation is the lone exception."[2]

In searching for answers, we're drawn to the social watershed that was the '60s. Today's generation of parents—and I'm among them—were the children who came of age at that time, vowing to discard the values of their parents, to eschew materialism, to forge a brave new world based on love, peace and freedom. Alas, the so-called summer of love that symbolized the free-spirit '60s has given root to the winter of regret that enslaves many a quarter-century later.

To its credit, the '60s generation has made a number of positive contributions to the country, confronting environmental dangers, racial discrimination and sexual inequality. This generation has dared to dream and explore. It has marched for peace, pioneered the computer revolution and sweated its way to new levels of physical fitness.

At the same time, however, it is dogged by painful paradoxes. To wit: The drugs and easy sex flaunted by the teenagers of the '60s have returned to haunt the children of those now-grown teenagers.

The same generation so critical of its parents has become the first generation of parents to be widely unavailable to its own children.

The same generation that once echoed The Beatles' "all-you-need-is-love" lyrics has become the most materialistic generation ever, complete with a prosperity-gospel twist that suggests wealth is some sort of divine right.

The same generation that exalts the intricate chain of ecology—protesting the demise of seals, snail darters and spotted owls—has turned its back on the intricate chain of human life that begins inside the womb.

The same generation that so fervently clamors for world peace is filled with people who can't find peace with the very person with whom they once chose to spend a lifetime.

I recently got a postcard from a Christian friend whose wedding my family had attended a decade earlier. For years, he had sent us postcards from the vacation spots he and his wife were enjoying. But this postcard was different. It had no picture of Big Ben or the Grand Canyon or The Caribbean at sunset. Instead, it was a plain postcard that said simply he and his wife were getting divorced.

The incident symbolizes the overriding contradiction

with baby boomers: The nation's largest, richest, healthiest and best educated generation—a generation full of hope, idealism and great expectations—is struggling to find personal contentment, particularly in its relationships.

Baby boomers, reported *Psychology Today* in two separate studies, are 10 times more likely to be depressed than their parents or grandparents.[3] They're five times as likely to be divorced as their parents.[4] In 1965, the city of 85,000 I recently moved from had only two marriage and family counselors listed in its Yellow Pages; 25 years later the book had 133, an increase that far surpassed its population increase.

What happened to the baby-boom generation? "We ended a war, toppled two presidents, desegregated the South, broke other barriers of discrimination," said California Congressman Tom Hayden. "How could we accomplish so much and have so little in the end?"[5]

In part, because, for all the energy expended on social and political change, the baby boom generation has shown little concern for consequences, cornerstones or commitment. We're the generation that saw clearly the cost-to-benefit ratio of the Vietnam War, but never stopped to appreciate the long-range effects of a seven-year-old being shuttled back and forth between divorced parents. The generation that exalted individual freedom at all costs, then found itself enslaved by a lack of boundaries. The generation that decided God was dead, then got addicted trying to find a replacement—whether the substitute was drugs, alcohol, work, money, food or fame.

In a poignant essay, novelist and former Secretary of the Navy James Webb wonders about what his generation will pass on to that of his off-to-college daughter. "The greatest legacy of the baby-boom generation's early adulthood has been that it asked all the right questions but resolved nothing . . . riven by disagreement, we have encouraged our children to believe that there are no touchstones, no true answers, no commitments worthy of sacrifice. That there are no firm principles. That for every cause there is a countercause. That for every reason to fight there is a reason to run."[6]

The generation's influence on American values cannot be overemphasized. Baby-boomers have restructured the economy, revived the health and fitness industry, molded the media, modified the morals. We've influenced the way people work, play, vote, buy, learn, worship and eat, the latter illustrated by a cartoon of a business woman standing in the microwave-food section of a supermarket. "Naw," she says, "I just don't feel like cooking tonight."

The Me Generation may look different than 25 years ago, but it is still very much alive, not only changing with the times, but often *changing* the times themselves. In the wake of the "revolutionary '60s," "the Me-Decade '70s" and the "self-indulgent '80s," the pattern is clear: The baby-boom generation, the proverbial pig in the python, is carving a new value system as it ages.

"The baby boom is, and will continue to be, the decisive generation in our history," wrote Landon Y. Jones, author of *Great Expectations: America & the Baby Boom Generation.*[7]

Against this backdrop, Christians find themselves challenged like never before. It is tempting to believe that those who have made personal commitments to Christ can quietly swirl in some protected eddy, removed from the rapids of a society that's crashing and tumbling toward some unforeseen destination. The reality is that we live in the mainstream and often ground on the same rocks as the rest.

Lives running on fast-forward. The cult of consumerism. Divorce. Drugs. Infidelity. Neglect. The percentages of Christians entrapped may be lower (though not by much), but the problems are the same. Just when you begin thinking you can seal yourself off from the world in your Christian cocoon, you learn of a faraway but close-to-your-heart couple—believers both—whose marriage is unraveling after one of them had an affair. Just when you believe that Christians are safe from evil, a friend at church tells you that her teenage son just entered a drug treatment program. Just when you think it only happens to the other family, the telephone rings. A cousin is dead. Suicide.

We rationalize that if we avoid the statistical snares—those "official" designations of defeat such as divorce—we've somehow "succeeded"; it is the same narrow notion underlying some people's belief that holiness is related exclusively to smoking, drinking and dancing. However, a lot of families who appear alive and well, in reality, are comatose—clinically alive but lacking any signs of the abundant life God intends for them.

Why? Because we've developed spiritual double vision, consciously conforming to Christ but subconsciously conforming to culture. Subtly seduced by everything from Madison Avenue to Me-ism, our priorities have become skewed, our values confused, our commitments compromised.

Take, for example, one of our culture's strongest undercurrents: materialism. In a church I used to attend, I knew a man who had a vibrant business, a happy family and an important role in the church. But as the man allowed his business to become more of a priority, everything else became less of a priority. He began dropping church responsibilities to spend more time on his business. Later, he began missing church to spend more time traveling on weekend business. Then he moved his family to another state so he could be closer to a major airport and travel more often on business.

Finally, he and his wife divorced. A family was split. Vows were broken. A commitment to Christ was neglected—all in the name of obsessively seeking an oasis that was only a cultural mirage.

As Christians, our lives too often reflect the have-it-all priorities of idols and self—idols reflected in such ways as materialism, trends, fantasy and freedom. And self-reflected in such ways as preoccupation with *our* needs, *our* image, *our* time and *our* rights.

What should our priorities be? God, not idols; others, not self. In Matthew 22:37-40, Christ makes it clear what we are to hold more dearly than all else: "Love the Lord your God with all your heart and with all your soul and with all your mind," he says, and "love your neighbor as yourself. All the Law and the Prophets hang on these two commandments."

If, near the end of our lives, we are to look back with contentment and not regret, we need to trade some cultural values for Christian values. But before we can do so, we need to develop a keen awareness of that culture's influence. Our values are so imperceptibly shaped that it's easy for our spiritual vision to become blurred without us even noticing. When my son recently got new lenses for his glasses, he was amazed at what he could see. "I had no idea what I couldn't see before," he said. Until he had his vision checked, he was unaware of how blurred it really was.

Consider this book something of a vision check. The journey through these pages is not intended as a guilt trip, no tour of spiritual shortcomings led by an infallible guide. Nor is it an expedition of baby-boom bashing led by a disgruntled member of the band. Instead, it is a cultural exploration led by someone who makes his living reporting on people— their lifestyles, their values, their choices. And a challenge for us all to seek solutions not from within, but from Him.

In the pages to come, you'll note two distinct approaches: Each of the 10 chapters shows how and why we must shed a particular cultural value. And each of the chapters concludes with two close-up stories about how such values— and God's values—play out in the lives of everyday people like you and me.

One story in particular comes to mind. I had interviewed a woman who had given up a lucrative and prestigious job to spend more time with her family; she and her husband were on the brink of divorce and her daughter was involved in drugs.

What she learned, she told me, was that people simply can't have it all. "And I don't particularly like that idea," she admitted.

But a question kept coming back to nag her, a question that ultimately triggered her decision to quit work, a question that she had to face when struggling to reach the American Dream.

"I said to myself, 'At what cost?' "

CHAPTER ONE

Trading Consumerism for Contentment

I once knew of two men who did not love thy neighbor, specifically each other. They lived next door to one another in large waterfront houses with emerald green lawns in a part of town so exclusive that—I kid you not—residents were known to have garage sales by appointment only. Both houses were worth a million dollars. From their living-room windows, the men could see sailboats and sunsets and mountains. You get the idea: These were not the type of guys who clipped 49-cent cornflakes coupons or checked phone booth coin returns for spare change.

At one point they were friends. But a laurel hedge came between them—literally and figuratively. It was on the property of the man we'll call Mr. Hedgeowner, and he loved it dearly. His neighbor, we'll call him Mr. Trimmer, did not love it dearly. He thought it obstructed his view so asked Mr. Hedgeowner to trim it. He refused.

So one day, when Mr. Hedgeowner was gone, Mr. Trimmer took his electric clippers and trimmed it himself. Mr. Hedgeowner was so angry, he told me, that his first instinct was to go next door with a baseball bat. Instead, he

gave Mr. Trimmer a stern warning to leave the hedge alone.
But a few months later, Mr. Trimmer trimmed it again. Mr.
Hedgeowner threatened to call the police.

Mr. Trimmer agreed to stop, but broke his promise.
This time, Mr. Hedgeowner did call the police. Mr. Trimmer
was arrested on charges of malicious mischief and criminal
trespass and hired an attorney. So did Mr. Hedgeowner. He
talked about suing Mr. Trimmer. The case dragged on.
Finally, almost a year later, it was legally resolved. But in
the minds of two men who seemingly had all that anyone
could want, I don't believe it was ever resolved.

Two men who seemingly had it all—deluxe-sized
American Dreams—and yet all the money and stocks and
bonds and $30,000 cars and lake views and boats and club
memberships and professional prestige could not compensate for what both men lacked: peace and contentment.

Money and things, we've come to believe, create a sort
of plexiglass shield able to deflect bullets of the real world.
Some learn the hard way that it just isn't so. Yet we live in a
consumer-oriented world where those who provide and
promote products desperately want us to keep believing
the myth. They fuel their own empty dreams by making
sure that our dreams are found in the things they sell. The
key to their contentment is making sure we don't find ours.
And even if we become satisfied with a product, Madison
Avenue is after us again, luring us with something new-
and-improved, an added option, a larger model—anything
to make us want more than we already have, or at least
want what our neighbor has.

Madison Avenue loves to see discontent, covetous-
ness, worry, comparison and blind ambition—all those
things that contradict God's values. People buy when
they're discontent, envious, afraid, left out and obsessed
with power or prestige. The materialism rampant in the
baby-boom generation is not so much a sign of success but
of desperation. Many have traded the pursuit of happiness
for the purchase of happiness.

To be sure, a life built on buying has its benefits. We live more comfortably, we have more options, we can gratify ourselves more immediately than before. But the price we pay is staggering. We easily become obsessed with things and lose sight of priorities. The "good life," as defined by so many new magazines, becomes a life based on food, wine, houses and travel—things, not people; goods, not God. Who needs a savior when I have a gold card? Why risk making a friend when I can buy a sound system that asks for nothing in return? Why build a wooden fort with the children's help when I can buy a plastic one by myself?

We become so entrenched with serving ourselves that we forget God calls us to serve Him and others. In 1988, a Gallup poll showed that Americans with low and moderate incomes were more generous with their dollars than Americans with high incomes; households with incomes below $10,000 gave an average of 2.8 percent of their incomes to charity while those with incomes between $50,000 and $75,000 gave only 1.5 percent. Money has a tendency to change our priorities. And yet followers of the new "prosperity gospel" would have us believe that it's God's will that we all become wealthy, comfortable, and wear only the finest clothes.

But God is much more interested in our character than in our comfort. "Seek first His kingdom and His righteousness; and all these things shall be added to you," Jesus said (Matthew 6:33). In the context of the verse, "these things" don't represent our heart's desires, but life's necessities.

The point isn't that poverty and spirituality are synonymous, but that we must be willing to allow God to be our foremost priority. When Jesus said that it is "easier for a camel to go through the eye of a needle than for a rich man to enter the kingdom of God" (Matthew 19:24) He implied that wealth can be a burden that prevents us from making God the priority He needs to be.

A pastor told me of a family who decided to buy a condominium in the mountains so they could ski more. Once they made the purchase, they felt an obligation to spend lots of time at the place. Activities and errands normally done on weekends began cluttering the weekday calendar. The family's time together fizzled. Church was out, period. "I'm not against condos," said the pastor, "but when a condo becomes the master of our time, energy and treasures, you can't serve the Lord."

What we purchase might not be as important as how we use what we purchase. I know a man and woman who own a beach cabin. They could have chosen to spend every weekend there. Instead, they visit it only periodically, usually as a means to gather with extended family members. And when they're not there? They allow friends and church groups from around the state to use it, meaning the cabin has become a place of ministry, not the master of their lives.

It's easy to point the finger at the wealthy to alleviate our own self-guilt about materialism. But materialism isn't reserved for those in an upper-tax bracket; it consumes anyone who becomes obsessed with the value of purchased goods at the expense of relationships or giving to others.

In a time when 40,000 children a day die of malnutrition and disease in Third World countries, 52 percent of Americans—people with the highest collective standard of living in the world—say they daydream about being rich.[1] How much is enough?

There is nothing innately evil about wanting to live in a nice house or buy a nice stereo system or purchase a nice car. But such niceties can become more than simple complements to the rest of our lives. In some cases, they *become* our lives. They can become the idols that we subconsciously worship, the priorities that nudge out our relationships, the replacements for something that's missing.

For some, products have become more than physical items. They have become surrogate saviors. While flipping through a friend's cable-TV channels, I came across a half-hour program devoted to promoting a single item—an iron. Curious, I watched as the audience oohed and ahhed when every feature was described or demonstrated. The host ballyhooed the iron with evangelical fervor. A woman came on stage and gave a personal testimony about how awesome this iron was; it would not scorch a shirt, it would not burn your hand, it was nothing short of a miracle, she said.

Indeed, as the show continued, I realized that this was more than a product advertisement, it was a consumerized church, Christ having been replaced by a non-scorching iron that would set us all free. At the end of the service, an altar call was given and, I presume that thousands of viewers around the country came forward with toll-free calls. They surrendered their Visa and Mastercard numbers to the operator and waited anxiously by the mailbox for the blessed coming of the promised one, the smoother of all wrinkles.

If you're like me, you've probably bought something that you were so enthusiastic about and that you'd waited so long for that you assumed it would change your life forever. Did it? Or did it, like the item I'm thinking about, eventually wind up being sold at a garage sale?

It's easy to say "money can't buy happiness"—but how many of us live as if we really believe it? A high-tech executive I interviewed unabashedly believed that contentment was only a credit-card buy away. "I thought I was having fun, taking exotic trips, buying Porsches, jewelry," she told me. "But they were like drugs. The more you did the more you needed it. You'd say, 'Last year I chartered a 55-foot boat so this year I better make it a 100-footer.' Money is like Chinese food: You eat it and an hour later, you're hungry."

If more money really equated to more fulfillment, why do so many people with sizable incomes still desperately search for satisfaction? Or use that money for destructive rather than constructive purposes? Sixteen percent of men earning less than $5,000 a year say they cheat on their wives. But of men who earn more than $70,000, 70 percent say they do. Fulfillment doesn't necessarily increase with the bank account.[2]

Interestingly, the more money we make, the more we think we need. People with household incomes under $10,000 say they need an average of $18,500 per year to get by. But people who make more than $50,000 a year believe they need an average of $75,000.[3] Certainly, some of us genuinely struggle to get by each week, but as *American Demographics* magazine points out, never have so many people been rich but think of themselves as poor.

Perhaps you're familiar with this American Express TV commercial: A couple is in an airport, having returned from vacation. "We were almost there," the woman says wistfully, as if to suggest that with a little more vacation time they could have broken through the gravity of real life and floated freely in carefree space. Now, they have arrived back at Reality International and life is once again a bummer.

Suddenly, they get an idea. Why not just pull out the American Express card and take off on another trip? Bingo, they're off, buying clothes, laughing, eating exotic food. The moral of the commercial? That you can get to the elusive land of fulfillment—you can get "there"—with a plastic card. The reality? That the exotic food they were eating was undoubtedly Chinese; half an hour later they were hungry. Guaranteed.

We think money can take us "there" but it can't. Five percent of Americans earning less than $15,000 a year say they have achieved the American Dream. What's interesting is that only 6 percent of those earning more than $50,000 say they have achieved it.[4] Money, it seems, is a mirage of contentment. Regardless of our income level, we think it can help us reach out and touch the coolness of an oasis. Unless we reach for the kingdom of heaven, however, we find only a dusty desert.

After years of climbing higher and higher in one of the country's most prestigious stockbrokerage firms, a Christian friend of mine was named manager of a big-city office. He'd waited a lifetime for such a position, but after two years, he was stressed like never before. "There was so much back-stabbing going on, people trying to get ahead, that I'd wake up every morning and vomit," he said.

He began praying about his job, began looking at it from not only his perspective, but God's perspective. Was this what life was really all about? He decided not, so he quit, taking a lower position with less pay, less prestige, less responsibility and, not incidentally, less stress. "It just wasn't worth it," he told me.

He had reached the oasis and found only a mirage. He had been part of a race where the quest to win superseded ethics, family, friendships. It's nothing new. "People who want to get rich fall into temptation and a trap and into many foolish and harmful desires that plunge men into ruin and destruction," Paul wrote two thousand years ago. "For the love of money is a root of all kinds of evil. Some people, eager for money, have wandered from the faith and pierced themselves with many griefs. But you, man of God, flee from all this, and pursue righteousness, godliness, faith, love, endurance and gentleness" (1 Timothy 6:9-11).

When we pursue such qualities, we're pursuing the author of such qualities—God. And in making Him a priority, other people become a priority. A teenager in my community was allowed to drive his father's new car to a prom. Rounding a corner, the car slid out of control, hit a curb and smashed into a building. Unhurt but emotionally devastated, the son called his father, who raced to the scene of the accident, quickly surveyed the situation and put his hand on his son's shoulder.

"You O.K.?" he asked. Later, an observer approached the father and asked him how he had been so calm about his new car being ruined.

"That's just a piece of metal," the man said. "My son's much more important than that."

Our challenge as Christians is to live daily with that same understanding of things and the same sense of urgency toward others. That might mean making some sacrifices. It might mean a woman staying home to raise children in a world that doesn't validate her role. It might mean being willing to dress less lavishly than those around us. It might even mean giving up a dream.

A retired man in my community was wrestling with whether he should join the local country club. He loved to play golf and, even though the membership fee was $20,000, he had the financial means to swing it. But after much prayer, he came up with a plan that left him at peace: He gave most of the $20,000 he'd saved to a missionary organization and decided to keep playing golf at a considerably less expensive public course.

Did he become a miserable, regretful man? No, because in giving he received. In carefully considering not what he wanted, but what God would want, he had seen more clearly his part in the kingdom.

In determining how we should approach spending and owning, we need to ask ourselves some questions. Will buying this item dilute time with family, friends, God? Can I realistically afford it? Why am I purchasing it? Am I buying something to keep pace with those around me? Because the advertisement seduced me? Because I have an unfulfilled need elsewhere in my life and, subconsciously, I'm hoping this will compensate?

Jesus can fill that need—continually. Materialism only temporarily quenches our thirst for fulfillment. Speaking to the Samaritan woman at the well, Jesus said, "Everyone who drinks this water will be thirsty again, but whoever drinks the water I give him will never thirst. Indeed, the water I give him will become in him a spring of water welling up to eternal life" (John 4:13-14).

The world's treasures are temporal; God's are eternal. "Do not store up for yourselves treasures on earth, where moth and rust destroy and where thieves break in and steal," Christ tells us. "But store up for yourselves treasures in heaven where moth and rust do not destroy, and where thieves do not break in and steal. For where your treasure is, there your heart will be also" (Matthew 6:19).

When our treasures are in heaven, when we have a sense of life as eternal, we don't have to "grab-for-all-the-gusto." We're free from the cultural tug to conform. Free from the frustration that causes grown men to let a laurel hedge block their friendship and lead to legal hassles. Finally, we're free to live more simple, other-oriented lives. That doesn't mean selling all that we own. It means owning without treasuring, possessing without being possessed. It means being content with what we have.

True contentment, said the Apostle Paul, does not depend on circumstances. "I have learned to be content whatever the circumstances. I know what it is to be in need, and I know what it is to have plenty. I have learned the secret of being content in any and every situation, whether well fed or hungry, whether living in plenty or in want. I can do everything through Him who gives me strength" (Philippians 4:11-13).

The choice is ours. We can attempt to get "there" with American Express and a couple of plane tickets. Or we can accept God's offer of contentment, which comes free and has no checkout time.

Safely Ashore

༄

*A*t age 41, he had wrapped prosperity around him as if it were a down comforter, guaranteed to stave off the biting wind of anything that might blow his way.

Like a 20th-century Horatio Alger character, he had risen from a small-town, middle-class background to acquire big-city clout. His income as a financial consultant exceeded $100,000 a year and he was in demand as a seminar speaker. He and his wife lived in a nice home in the safe environs of suburbia. The two of them vacationed in Europe and cruised the Caribbean.

None of which mattered to the man now. Alone in his den on a rainy February afternoon, he wept uncontrollably.

Forgotten were all the evenings he had spent punching the numbers on the calculator, making sure he and his wife's nest egg was secure. Forgotten were all the days at the office, boldly beating back the competition to fortify his financial fortress.

The master of his own universe was in the throes of a nervous breakdown.

All along, he had been expecting the enemy to come from somewhere else—a flat market, an underestimated competitor, a jealous employee. Instead, he would soon learn, the enemy had attacked from within.

In his parents' eyes, this would be the ultimate disgrace: a grown man crying. He had been raised to believe that, regardless of your vulnerabilities, you never let 'em see you sweat. Appearance was everything. His mother masked her inferiority complex by dressing in perfect outfits and keeping an immaculate lawn and garden. His father masked his insecurities by attaching his identity to work and little else.

"I was raised in a Christian home," said the man, "but there's a difference between preaching values and living values, between operating a life of faith and living by a bunch of slogans."

After he was involved in a sledding accident as a boy, he got so much special treatment from his parents that he became spoiled. He found it hard to make friends. And he made himself a promise: *I'll show them. When I grow up I'm going to make a lot of money and be successful.*

He worked his way through college. Afterward, he sold insurance and ultimately got into financial consulting.

He got married but it was a stormy relationship from the beginning. Like his parents, he lived a dual life. "I preached Christian principles," he said, "but I didn't live them."

He didn't want any children; he was too selfish. Instead, he amassed more and more money. He stretched his work day regularly to 10 and 12 hours. He became irritable and insensitive to others, particularly to his wife. She called him King Tut.

"I operated on fear," he says. "Fear that I would lose my business and my prestige."

But, remembering a cue from his past, he nevertheless tried to smile at all times. He bought only tailor-made suits for the same reason his mother wore only the finest clothes. He bragged of his accomplishments. His list of clients became more and more prestigious. People became tools, things that he could manipulate to get what he wanted.

Though he wasn't averse to spending money, he wasn't addicted to it, either. Unlike yuppies, spending money wasn't his security; *having* it was. He would go home in the evenings, sit in his den and crunch the numbers, making sure his protection was there. He would analyze the situation, plan the moves needed to strengthen his stronghold.

"I was always trying to reassure myself," he says.

The more money he made, the more invulnerable he felt and the less he felt he needed anyone else, particularly God. Work, accumulate, analyze, plan. Work, accumulate, analyze, plan. The pattern continued for years and years, until he found himself getting depressed more often and more easily. He dreaded going to work. He couldn't sleep. He was on the brink of divorce.

Finally, on that afternoon in the den, the man crumbled from the inside out. The nervous breakdown lasted for months, though he continued to work. He would find himself crying uncontrollably, rolling on the floor, mentally tortured by his own thoughts. Perhaps he should just end his life; what good had he brought anyone? The regret about his selfishness ate away at him like acid. Once, his wife came home from work and found him in the middle of the street, yelling at the top of his lungs, "God, forgive me!"

"Compared to a nervous breakdown," he says, looking back, "depression is a trip to Disneyland."

He describes it as fishing from a boat in the middle of a lake, knowing you're unable to swim. There are no life jackets aboard and suddenly the boat springs a leak. The water starts rising, first to your ankles, then to your knees, then to your neck. Finally, you sink—only to find that you're only in four feet of water.

But after the torment came the tenacity to change, the courage to overcome the past. For all its pain, the breakdown had forced the man to examine his life for what it really was, not what he pretended it to be. What he saw wasn't pretty—a selfish, insecure man who professed to follow Christ but refused to give Him control.

A Christian counselor helped him understand himself, why he had become who he was and how he could change. He immersed himself in God's word, particularly the Psalms. He realized that God would forgive his selfishness. And he prayed fervently.

The result was something akin to a summer rain that freshens a 12-week drought. "What I realized is that it's not important what I accomplish," he says. "What's important is who I am. My priorities have changed. I realized that what's really important isn't my business or my money, but my relationship with God and my wife. Money can be more curse than blessing."

He's cut back his time at work considerably. People who know him say he's more willing to show his vulnerabilities instead of hiding them behind a tailored suit; more willing to admit a mistake than blame someone else. He's more sincere. More empathetic. And less manipulative of those around him.

He's developed a core of Christian friends who aren't just people to socialize with, but people who genuinely care about him. He's also developed a clearer understanding of what fulfillment is all about. Prosperity, he's learned, is not what we own or how much money we make, but what we have inside us. "There's a big difference between happiness and joy," he says. "Happiness is self-centered and depends on circumstances; joy is other-centered and rises above circumstances. Happiness is superficial; joy is deep."

Once, he thought fulfillment was his—and his alone—to create and protect. "What saved me," he says, "was finally being forced to look at myself in the mirror."

Only then, with God's grace, was he able to get safely ashore from the middle of the lake.

Street of Dreams

ই৯

Two women were standing in the den of the 5,600-square-foot, $590,000 Excalibur, one of 10 houses in a Street of Dreams show.

"Where's the ladder to reach the books on the top shelf?" asked one.

"Who cares?" said the other. "Just ring for the butler."

By the end of the month-long show, more than 100,000 people will have toured this pocket of posh. They will see the nanny's suite in one house. Feel the elegance of the circular entrance way in another. Hear the music from the outdoor underground speakers in yet another.

These are the kinds of houses most of us envision only in our dreams. And, collectively, they form a neighborhood that smacks of some sort of magic kingdom.

But if alluring, their glamor and glitz are also deceptive. What none of the builders' brochures reminds us is that a home is more than color schemes, bay windows and quadraphonic stereo systems.

The most important ingredient is people. Relationships. Families.

That's easy to forget as you tour the Street of Dreams. The houses, without a doubt, are stunning. And as you see the custom-etched windows and king-sized closets, you find yourself starting to believe that, yes, luxury and large rooms are the keys to contentment, the guarantees of The Good Life, the very essence of The American Dream.

The couples who move into these houses will never argue, their teenagers will never take drugs and their dogs will never bark in the night.

What we tend to forget is that houses are nothing more than stages where people play their parts.

The point isn't that there's something innately wrong with large homes, sprawling lawns and bubbling spas. Or that plush neighborhoods are necessarily void of contented people.

But such places aren't the *guarantees* of contentment we might think they are. Recently, as I wound my way up to the show's hillside setting, I passed a neighborhood of expensive houses. A year ago I had read about a woman who lived in one of those houses. Unable to find peace in the world, she had jumped from a bridge to end her search.

In the end, where she lived could not protect her from how she lived. Our need for fulfillment and acceptance respects no geographic boundaries; we crave them wherever we call home.

Walking through the Street of Dreams, it's easy to think of this architectural wonderland as some sort of fortress against the real world. It is not. The Street of Dreams is also The Street of Reality. On The Street of Dreams, families will argue, children will take drugs, dogs will bark in the night.

So what about those of us who don't live in such settings? Can we find happiness in our less grandiose houses, where the family room is also the den, the sewing room and the "temporary home"—going on four years now—of the papier-mache Mount St. Helens replica? Where the back lawn might have a baseball diamond worn into it? Where the shower might need regrouting?

Yes, because a home is not wood and walls and glass and tile. It's people. Some modest houses are actually rich homes. And some rich houses are actually broken homes. Again, where we live is much less important than how we live—and who we live for. Likewise, what we own is less important than the priority we give to what we own.

In the final analysis, what's more important—that our house is large, or that the people inside are close?

That we have a state-of-the-art intercom system, or that we actually communicate as a family?

That our kitchen is straight from *Architectural Digest*, or that we make time to eat together in that kitchen?

Houses are wonderful places. Streets of Dreams can be inspiring. But regardless of where we live, the challenge is the same for us all: Realizing that a house is not necessarily a home. And dreams are built not with a hammer, but with the heart.

CHAPTER TWO

Trading
Fast Forward
for Play
and Pause

B ob Simon, the CBS news correspondent taken captive by Iraqi forces during the Persian Gulf War, experienced something few of us ever will. Not only did he endure a life-threatening ordeal but he was given a rare opportunity to put his life in perspective. After being freed, he told reporters that during his weeks in waiting, all the history he had seen as a journalist meant far less to him than his relationships.

"What came back to me," he told The Associated Press, "was not the last day of Saigon, or (Anwar) Sadat coming to Israel or these things. What came back to me is the first time I carried my daughter into the Mediterranean. . . . The day I took a bicycle trip through the French countryside to flirt with this young French girl who was to become my wife. Stuff that had nothing to do with history or news or journalism."[1]

It's interesting how we view life so very differently when we're in danger of losing it. How sometimes it takes tragedy to refocus what's important. How sometimes it takes separation—even for a weekend trip—to make us appreciate the people we're apart from.

But if such times remind us what's really important, why do our day-to-day lives often reflect the opposite? If we took a serious look at our schedules—where we spend most of our time—we'd have to conclude that what's really important is work, entertainment, television, travel, recreation and errands. That the essence of life is not building relationships, but accomplishing a seemingly endless amount of things in a finite amount of time.

Why? Because, in a cultural Catch-22, we're so busy living that we don't have time to reflect on life. Time, it seems, is the tyrant of the '90s, the great paradox: Each day we get the same amount of it and yet we never seem to have enough of it.

Family conversation is on the endangered list. The average married couple spends four minutes a day in meaningful conversation. Houses have become transit stations, places to grab a bite and leave a message on the refrigerator before taking off to another destination. The family meal is a vanishing species. Only roughly a third of U.S. families gather seven days a week for dinner. Another third gather three nights or less.[2]

This is the age of the *One-Minute Parent*, the two-minute hamburger, the 10-minute lube job, the 20-minute tan. The age of instant food and instant gratification, Zap mail and zippy copies, quick fixes and quick faxes. With our breakneck pace, we don't have time to even *see* the roses, much less stop and smell them.

We've sanctified a rushed pace as having a sort of inherent virtue, as if going someplace fast is naturally good. But the question lost in our almost panic-driven pursuit is this: Just where are we trying to get? It's as if *where* we're going becomes insignificant. What's important is that we just go, go, go. And so, lemming-like, that's what we do.

In a world of fast-forward, we desperately need to hit pause and play. There are some things which cannot be rushed: time with God, time with family, time with friends, time with ourselves.

I learned something about the effects of rushing through life early one dark January morning. For weeks, I'd been staying up late working on a freelance writing project that I never should have accepted because I was already too busy. As I bolted out the door, I was not only tired, but 15 minutes away from a church leadership meeting that started in five.

I mentally grumbled; the car's windshields were frosted over so I had to scratch a small hole in the ice to see out. I should have poured warm water over the windshield or waited until the defroster kicked into action, but I didn't have time.

Approaching an intersection, I saw the green blur of a traffic light and started to turn left. Suddenly, I realized I had no idea where the street was. I could see nothing. I slammed on the brakes. In that single instant, months of pushing the limits of time took its toll. The car bounced up on a curb and straddled the sidewalk. It came to rest just in front of a telephone pole that would have creased the front left of the car like an aluminum can crinkled against a crow bar.

It happened so fast that I didn't have time, like Bob Simon, to reflect on what was important in life. But afterward, I realized how devastating racing blindly through life can be. In a sense, I'd been fortunate; I'd gotten off with a "warning." For others, the penalty can be more serious: a physical breakdown, a relational breakdown, a spiritual breakdown.

Once, while walking along the Oregon Coast with my then five-year-old son, I pointed to two massive rocks, each about the size of a recreational vehicle. "Those rocks were once connected together and were one big rock," I said. "But they split apart."

My son looked at the two rocks. "I didn't hear any-thing," he said. As adults, we can snicker at our children's lack of perspective on time. And yet if they don't under-stand the big picture, sometimes neither do we. We often seem oblivious to the cost of our constant rushing.

- ❧ Hurrying means losing perspective. When we're so wrapped up in the stuff of life, we're too close to see the big picture. It's like looking closely at a screened photograph: all you see are fuzzy shades of gray. But when you take time to stand back, that tiny dot pattern becomes a picture with distinct blacks and whites. It becomes an image with mean-ing, a picture with a message. When was the last time you stepped back and surveyed the picture of your life?

- ❧ Hurrying means losing touch with those around you. Time is the soil in which relationships grow. Without time, our links to family, friends and God all wither. Children take patience. Spouses take a listening ear. Friendships take follow through. God takes our day-to-day attention.

- ❧ Hurrying means creating hurried children. Too many kids today are growing up without a child-hood, forced to program their days as if they were pint-sized executives. We need to slow them down and allow them the innocence of youth, not push them into the adulthood that will come soon enough without our prodding.

- ❧ Hurrying means overlooking the value of processes. We have shifted from being a process-oriented cul-ture to a results-oriented culture. Strapped for time, we pay a fast-food restaurant to feed our family. We pay a child-care center to nurture our children. Some even pay a store clerk to do their gift shopping.

I once interviewed a woman who cooked everything on a wood stove, grilled pancakes from scratch and made pies with apples she picked herself. I explained that she could be doing this much faster if she would use a microwave oven and store-bought mixes. With an irresistible "look-here-sonny" expression, she said, "If I don't have time to cook, then I don't have time to live."

Buying a loaf of bread or eating at McDonald's or having someone else watch our children isn't necessarily wrong. But when secondhand giving becomes the rule, rather than the exception, we've lost sight of something important: that the value of giving is not only in the finished product, but in the process that made it.

Though I've received many cash Christmas bonuses over the years, I can't remember a single thing I've purchased with those bonuses. But I will never forget the wooden clipboard given to me by an editor. Why? It wasn't that I'd been waiting my whole life for a clipboard; for $2.99 I could have bought one myself. What made that present special was the process by which it came to me. It had not been picked up from the five-and-dime on an 11th-hour shopping trip; it had been handcrafted especially for me. It had been planned: first the idea, then the design, then the choice of different laminated woods. It had been custom crafted. What meant the most was that this busy man—a man who was forever winging his way across the country—had set aside time specifically for me.

Do we do that with our friends, our spouses, our children—set aside time specifically for them? Our culture, at least with children, gives us little support for such a lifestyle. And that does not bode well either for the current generation of children or the one to come. Psychologists say that children who lack attention seek to fill their lack of esteem through material possessions and achievements. Many mothers and fathers are only too happy to heap possessions on their children and encourage achievement to alleviate the guilt they feel for their lack of involvement. The result? We create a generation nurtured not on love but on objects, not on relationships but on accomplishments.

What really impresses our children isn't our job title or annual salary or club memberships, but our willingness to play Crazy-Eights with them, listen to them and look them in the eye. To hold them when they hurt. To tuck them in and listen to their prayers and to explain to them all the mysteries of life, like why God made the wind invisible.

So, is the answer "quality time," that lingering buzz-phrase from the '80s? Yes and no. Yes, because time with our children should be first-rate. No, because quality time is not enough. If quality time were sufficient, why not utilize it in schools and business? Let's send our children to school only one day a week—but let's make it a *quality* day. Let's open the supermarket only four hours a day, but let's make them four *quality* hours. The fact that we're unwilling to use the same argument for any other part of our lives suggests something about our culture's priorities.

We often rationalize that we can compensate for our lack of time with the family; after a fast-paced winter we can all take a vacation. That approach only looks good on paper. As a former distance runner, I remember our coach emphasizing keeping an even pace. If you go too hard, he said, you won't have energy for later on. If you go too easy, you'll lose touch with the others and be unable to compensate with a last-minute burst. The former suggests that sprinting in our day-to-day lives will ultimately leave us worthless to our teammates; the latter suggests that by the time the vacation rolls around, a last-minute kick won't be enough to make up for the time and distance that's been lost.

Long ago, wooden toys were intricately handcrafted with time and care by their maker; as a result, they were functional, creative and sturdy. Today, plastic toys are created by rapid-armed robots on assembly lines; as a result, they are fragile and rarely last. In our fast-paced approach to our children, have we become assembly-line parents instead of handcrafting parents? Are we producing fragile children because of it?

As husbands and wives, are we taking the time with our spouses to help build something that will last? As friends, are we finding room in our busy schedules for people who hurt? As followers of Christ, are we taking the time to absorb His word and seek His guidance?

"Be still," we're told, "and know that I am God" (Psalm 46:10).

The key to solving the time crisis is, first, to make sure we have time for Him. Only when we're closely connected with God can we hope to be closely connected with those around us. A relationship with Him shows us what's important in life and what's not, what we should add to our schedule and what we should cut.

Nobody's suggesting we smother our children with our presence, but either we're there to help meet their needs or they'll find replacements who will. Children do not come with easy-to-assemble instructions. They take time.

In a newspaper story on hospices—places that take care of the dying—the program's director was asked how a hospice volunteer contributes most. It wasn't the person's medical knowledge, ability to lift patients or personality. It was, she said, the person's willingness to *be there when they were needed*. Children don't need parents to hover over them. What they need is parents who are like the hospice volunteer: willing to be there when needed.

My wife and I have a long list of people we'd like to have over for dinner, but by the time we get around to inviting some of them it's too late; they've moved or we've moved. We can't simply make promises to ourselves and others. At some point, we need to act. At some point, we need to quit making excuses, clear our schedules and *serve our customers*.

Cutting back on commitments is not easy. We risk hurting people we care about, feeling as if we're letting the church down, allowing a co-worker to outperform us. But would we rather risk having an accident more serious than the one in my car I described earlier? It may be a drug dependency. A divorce. A fractured friendship. A spiritual wreck from which we'll never recover.

Like the distance runner, we need to pace ourselves. Slow down and analyze how we spend our time and what it says about our values. Remember the importance of rest. Even God, after creating the world, took a break. And block off time for God, family and friends just like we block off time for work, meetings and racquetball.

When interviewing Steve Largent, the record-setting ex-Seattle Seahawks wide receiver, what impressed me most wasn't his commitment to football but his commitment to his family. Every Friday night, he had a cast-in-stone date with his wife; every Saturday morning, he devoted to the family. Without that kind of prioritizing, it's easy to neglect the people we love.

After a particularly busy winter, I remember seeing bare tree limbs contrasted against a clear, late-afternoon sky. I stared at them in wonder, as if I'd never seen a tree in my life. For months, I had been too busy to even notice trees, much less the striking contrast of gnarly branches silhouetted against an April sky. I couldn't help but wonder what else I had missed as this season of my life came and went. Had I really been there to listen—really listen—to my wife's concerns? To share in my children's joys? To join in my friends' struggles?

Plenty of people in their twilight years have wished they could wind back the hands of time and take their teenager to a ball game. They've longed to take an evening walk with a spouse who's since died or to see the unbridled joy of a child running through a summer sprinkler.

But nobody, while lying on his death bed, ever wished he'd spent more time at the office.

No Second Chances

ે

*W*e *shuffle along,* past the coin collections and pocket watches and jewelry, to documents and small items sealed in plastic bags. It's all unclaimed property, waiting to be auctioned, the forgotten or overlooked possessions of owners now gone.

War medals, diplomas, children's report cards...

The items once sat in 1,500 safe deposit boxes in banks across the state. But the owners never returned for them. For most, time ran out. They died and had no heirs.

Rosaries, letters, train tickets...

Under state law, such contents are considered abandoned if they go unclaimed for five years after the rental period of the box expires. The state tries to find the owners. If unsuccessful, a public auction is held three years after the property is received. And that's why they're on display at this auction preview.

Boy Scout patches, a receipt from the Kuhio Hotel in Waikiki and a child's color-crayon drawing of a bunny rabbit...

This is the stuff that people once deemed too valuable to keep at home, where it might be stolen, burned or misplaced. Now, it sits on a table, sealed in plastic, waiting for the highest bidder.

Insurance policies, bank books, comic books...

Each bag is a mystery, the clues doing more to arouse curiosity than solve the case. The bags may be three or four inches thick, but only a few items on the top and bottom are visible. In one you find the immigration papers of Udolf Matschiner, who arrived at Ellis Island in 1906. Did he find what he was looking for in America?

Dog tags, draft cards, discharge papers...

Thomas Curran enlisted in the U.S. Army on Feb. 7, 1892, at Fort Meade, S.D. He was 25 years old. Did he wind up fighting in the Spanish-American War? And what became of Charles W. Herwig, who got an honorable discharge from the Army two months after the Japanese surrender? Did he marry? Have a family? Buy a home in the suburbs?

Two marbles, three stones and a belt buckle...

The items are together in one bag. That's all. Why these things? Do they represent some special memory, some special person?

Passports, telegrams, newspaper clippings...

A yellowed, 1959 article from a Santa Ana, Calif., newspaper is headlined, *Vlahovich's mother sobs at 'guilty' verdict*. A mother's son had been convicted of murder. The mother wept, pleading with the judge to spare her son. "Take my blood," she screamed. "Kill *me*."

What happened to that mother? Did she ever get over the pain of seeing her son led away to jail? Or to die? What was his sentence? Is he still in jail? Still alive?

Matchbooks, undeveloped film, a mining claim . . .

On Oct. 26, 1927, James McDonald had been granted a one-year claim on gold near Dawson Creek in the Yukon Territory. How much did he find? What did he use the gold to get? Did he know Robert Service? Did gold bring him fulfillment? Peace? Contentment?

Birth certificates, marriage certificates, divorce papers, last wills and testaments . . .

The official business of life intermingled with the unofficial business of life—a lock of blonde hair, a child's math paper and a poem called "Grandmother's Attic," typed on a typewriter with a sticky "e."

> *While up in Grandmother's attic today*
> *In an old red trunk neatly folded away*
> *Was a billowy dress of soft old grey*
> *Of rose brocade were the panniers wide*
> *With quilted patterns down the side*
> *And way in the back against the wall*
> *Of the little old trunk was an old silk shawl*
> *Silver slippers, a fan from France*
> *An invitation to a dance*
> *Written across the program blue*
> *Was "Agatha dear, may I dance with you?"*

It was as if those of us at the auction preview have been allowed entry into hundreds of Grandmother's Attics, the attics of unknown people.

Once, long ago, those children's drawings and war medals and marbles meant something to someone; now they are vacuum-sealed vestiges of lives come and gone, bags of memories that a stranger will buy.

Diaries, photographs, the ink print of a newborn's feet . . .

In the wake of death, most of the items speak volumes about life. They also suggest a sense of finality, a realization that life on earth ends, and certain things are left behind.

What will we leave behind? What legacy will we pass on to our children? What are we investing in now that will pay dividends even after we're gone?

Time comes. Time goes. There are no second chances.

Lost and Found

ꝫ

A year ago, I sat on the same sofa in the same house and talked with the same teenager.

On that warm September afternoon, he had spoken slowly, almost incoherently. He was eating a carton of ice cream with a spoon. He weighed about 100 pounds, hadn't showered in a week, had hair to his shoulders and bags under his eyes.

The previous night he had tried killing himself. He was 15 years old, a cocaine dealer hooked on his own product.

Seeing him today, I could barely believe the change. He bounced in the door, fresh from school, where he's among the top 10 percent in his class. Thanks to a new diet and weight training, he had bulked up to 145 pounds. His hair was short and stylish. He spoke enthusiastically and had landed a job. But the biggest change was one that I didn't pinpoint until sometime later: He laughed.

This is a story about beating drugs. About a kid who, in all likelihood, was going to wind up dead, but now is very much alive. About a fast-lane father and mother too busy making money to notice they were losing their son. About a family once fragmented but now back together.

When I first wrote about the boy, nothing I'd ever written provoked as much response. Readers were stunned at the situation. "I was doing $2,000 to $3,000 a day," said the boy.

What shocked people was that this was no street kid. This was a suburban kid. He was your neighbor, my neighbor, a kid who lived in a split-level home with a Porsche in the garage, in a neighborhood where people cut their grass on Saturday mornings and barbecue on Saturday nights.

Frustrated, his father had called me at the newspaper where I was a columnist. He wanted other parents to understand the power—and pervasiveness—of cocaine.

Shortly after the article ran, the son was arrested for cocaine possession. "I'd gone from hopes and dreams to watching my son be led away in handcuffs," his father said.

The youth went to a local drug rehabilitation center, but was asked to leave when dealers started pestering him. The parents sent him to a nonvoluntary rehab center in another state.

"That was the toughest day of my life," said the father. "He just kept crying and holding his dog."

The plan didn't work. The boy came home and again got involved in drugs. Meanwhile, though, his father—with prompting from his wife—was doing something he had put off time after time: facing his own shortcomings, his own addiction.

He entered a treatment center, stopped drinking and started understanding why his son may have rebelled. His son later entered the same facility, and came out with a new perspective, too.

Together, they started to do some sorting out. Among other things, they found a son who basically was on his own as a teenager because his parents were wedded to work. Together, they made more than $100,000 a year, the mother working long hours, the father on the road Monday through Friday.

"Why wasn't I around?" asked the father. "Because I'm an American. I make money. Big money."

The two also discovered a father who wanted to be everything to his son that *his* alcoholic father had not been to him, a father who perhaps pushed too hard to make big money—and pushed too hard to make his son the All-American athlete.

The son's rebellion was to switch from playing sports to selling drugs, an arena in which he quietly competed against his father. "I thought I was better than him," said the son. "I mean, I made more money in a weekend than he could make in a month. I emotionally destroyed him."

Finally, reconciliation. "He used to push me," said the son. "Now he meets me halfway. That's created a bond. I look up to him. I'd like to be like him."

Said the father: "I've learned there are a lot of things that are more important than materialism and working every waking hour of the day." He now has a new job that doesn't require him to travel all week. "We have some quiet time now to get to know each other again."

No family goes overnight from drug addiction to *Cosby*. No wounds heal without a scar. This family isn't recovered, but it's recovering. Shadowed by that reality, this is still a different boy—and a different family—than the one I'd seen a year ago.

"Whatever hasn't killed this family has made it stronger," said the boy.

The family recently went to a movie together, a seemingly ho-hum experience for some but "unheard of for us," according to the father. They've taken long walks on the beach. And the father and son have bought motorcycles and ride together regularly.

"He says, 'Be careful' to me every time I leave the house," said the son.

A few weeks ago, the father had a birthday. What he got from his son wasn't a tie or a shirt. It was a poem from the boy whom he'd once seen writhing in a hospital emergency room after a drug overdose, the boy whom he'd once seen in handcuffs. It ended like this:

> *Thank you for helping me*
> *Through the years*
> *and crying with me*
> *when I shed my tears*
>
> *You have meant so much*
> *to me each day*
> *sorry it took*
> *so long to say.*

CHAPTER THREE

Trading Trends for Tradition

In the spring of 1991, a *Time* magazine cover story announced that Americans were shifting back to macaroni and cheese, family reunions and push-it-yourself lawn mowers. Having it all was out; homier values were in. Fast-track careers were out; family was in.

On the surface, it was a story that many of us could feel good about. And yet America has become so meteoric in its social trends that you wondered how deep the commitment really was and how long it would really last. Our values have changed so rapidly in the last 25 years that you wondered if this were just another social wind that will soon blow another direction.

Nothing escapes the clutches of trendiness these days, including God. "Spirituality is in," said theologian Martin Marty of the University of Chicago.[1] Environmentalism is in. Even volunteerism, as untrendy a pursuit as seems possible, has succumbed to the world of fad, thanks largely to Hollywood. "Last year, chic charities fought Ethiopian famines and drug abuse," said *American Demographics* magazine. "This year, the homeless are hot."[2]

Such trends have the potential to rally much-needed support for good causes. But they also have the potential to cheapen the causes themselves. Consider the back-to-the-family trend. One magazine, in suggesting that families were now a "star attraction," used as evidence the increase in Father's Day sales, particularly in the area of ties, cuff links and wallets.

Reality isn't like that. The barometer for the health of the American family isn't found in cuff-link sales, magazine spreads and TV sitcoms, but in what's going on in the real homes of real families like yours and mine. While I'm all for families becoming more valued, I'm also aware that "star attractions" usually enjoy a brief existence; today's hot singer is tomorrow's has-been. Today's fad is tomorrow's garage-sale special.

What the American family needs is not to become trendy, but to remain a tradition. The family needs to be a day-to-day, week-to-week, year-to-year priority, not something we commit to because some Hollywood star has endorsed it or it makes good dinner-party conversation.

Commitment can be deceptive. On Earth Day, 1990, an estimated 750,000 people came to Central Park in New York to show their support for the environment. That's the good news. The bad news is that they left 100 tons of trash. Just how deep was their commitment to the environment?

Almost overnight, product manufacturers have become chest-beating environmental crusaders. Suddenly, virtually every dish soap is environmentally safe. Every paint is nontoxic. Every package is biodegradable. Given the sorry state of our environment, that's wonderful news. But five years from now, when the bloom is off the environmental bud, will product manufacturers still be making such boasts? Are they genuinely concerned about the environment—or simply doing whatever it takes to get people to buy their products?

Likewise, are we embracing certain values—God, family, a simpler lifestyle—because we're genuinely committed to them or because we fear being left off the back-to-the-basics bandwagon?

It's encouraging that baby boomers are returning to church. But to embrace God because "spirituality is in" is to suggest that the creator of the universe is some sort of Cabbage Patch Doll with secret powers. Our consumer-oriented culture seems to want a user-friendly God who places no demands on His followers. Are we falling for this airbrushed version of God? Are we turning to Him because it's the "thing to do" or because we realize He is Lord of all? Will our commitment to Him deepen with time or fade with the fad?

We live in an impatient culture that flits from one fad to another as people search for fulfillment. Naturally, each of us goes through phases in life in which our interests change. But when we're constantly jumping from one trend to another, it signals not simply a decision to try something new, but a desperate search to find something meaningful. That's because while God-based traditions can bring fulfillment, man-based trends cannot. They work for a while; but only for a while.

Traditions, of course, aren't inherently positive; they are simply established thoughts, actions or behaviors handed down from one generation to another. It was once traditional in this country to own slaves, deny women the right to vote and cut down trees with no thought of replacing them.

Nevertheless, many traditions *are* good. Traditions reinforce our values, focus our lives, put things in perspective. When we hear the organ playing "The Wedding March," we're immediately reminded of our own vows. Of the sacredness of marriage. Of the importance of what is about to take place.

And yet when it comes to tradition, America has been doing more clearcutting than selective thinning in the past

25 years, leaving behind a scarred hillside that can no longer be ignored. Judeo-Christian values, the nuclear family and individual responsibility—traditional threads that have bound this culture for centuries—have been leveled, leaving few moral absolutes, lots of hurting families and an excess of individual freedom that ultimately hurts the common good.

In the '60s, baby boomers decreed that the nuclear family was an unnecessary arm of the establishment and so went about changing it. But after more than two decades of experimenting with everything from communes to cohabitation to open marriage to contractual marriage, the results have been disappointing.

Among the fallout has been fathers and children engaged in weekend-only relationships, grandparents cut off from their grandchildren because of divorce and single mothers trying to do the job of two people. Many children today are growing up in a values vacuum because the traditions of family and faith have been discarded or forgotten.

A woman recently called the newspaper where I work to point out a mistake she had made while filling out a wedding announcement form. She had written that her fiancé's parents were dead. "Actually," she told me, "they're alive."

Curious, I asked why she had thought they were dead. "Oh, my fiancé never mentioned them and so I just assumed they were," she said.

Granted, this represents a worst-case scenario of family apathy. But even on a broader base, family traditions are being severely diluted. A high school senior in a wealthy suburb surprised some people in our community when, during her graduation speech, she posed some questions to parents: ". . . We wonder why we live in so many one-parent homes, why so many parents are abandoning us? What has happened to long walks and longer talks, going to church on Sunday and eating dinner at Grandma and Grandpa's house?"[3]

In our trend-oriented times, it was a cry for tradition, a plea for roots, a reminder that life's simple things are still important to young people.

One in four children now live in a single-parent home. Two of every five American women giving birth to their first child are not married when they became pregnant. Half of all teenagers drink regularly. More than a million teen-age girls get pregnant each year. And half of all marriages end in divorce. If this is the "new tradition"—and, sadly, it's becoming so—then we must commit ourselves to maintaining the old. Our cultural answer to problems is changing the system instead of changing ourselves. Nobody's suggesting, for example, that the family is an infallible institution. What needs fixing, however, is not the structure itself but us—the people within that structure.

Sociologist William Donohue refers to polls that show overwhelming support for "more emphasis on traditional family ties;" in one, 86 percent of those sampled said they would welcome such a shift. Yet when asked whether people desire a "return to traditional standards regarding sexual relations," only 21 percent said yes.

"It seems nearly everyone yearns for the ties that traditional family living provide," wrote Donohue, chairman of the sociology department at LaRoche College in Pittsburgh, "but few are willing to make the sacrifices that are necessary to achieve such a status. Or in today's vernacular, we want to experience the solidarity that the Waltons exhibit while living the life of 'Miami Vice.' "[4]

Those who keep a close eye on American values say the '90s will be a time for "deeper things." In a *Parents* magazine poll, 78 percent of the respondents expressed a desire to return to "traditional values and old-fashioned morality." But the desire to return to something and actually returning are two different things. "Wisdom is proved right by her actions," Jesus said (Matthew 11:19).

In our extended family, it has become traditional for the children to put on a Christmas Eve pageant/talent show. This is not exactly Broadway quality stuff, particularly when Joseph is wearing Nikes. But to see children act out the Christmas story has, for me, become one of the most meaningful, thought-provoking times of the season.

Some people recharge their faith each year with a traditional retreat, either alone or with others. It's a time to examine their lives, where they've been and where they're going. If you spend time with God daily, you're establishing a tradition of sorts that can fortify your faith. In simply attending church, you're creating a tradition, making a statement, subtle though it may be, that this is a priority in your life.

To make tradition a priority does not mean living in the past, nor does it mean denying the reality that the world shifts and that, in some ways, we need to shift with it. But we also need to remember God's tradition for meeting our needs, for making good on His promises, for giving us the day-to-day power of the Holy Spirit that transcends man's quick-fix solutions. "Stand firm and hold to the teachings we passed on to you, whether by word of mouth or by letter," Paul wrote (2 Thessalonians 2:15).

Trends ask that we follow the whims of the world; tradition that we follow the Lord of the world. What steps are you taking to anchor your lives in tradition instead of blindly following trends?

Tradition means staying beside the person you married when culture encourages divorce. Considering the needs of the common good in a culture that heralds individual freedom. Clinging to God's ways when culture promotes people's ways. Holding to the traditional value of moral absolutes in a world that wants them voided. And committing to God, to those around us and to simplicity of living not because it's suddenly vogue, but because such choices are what make life worth living.

Just because we have not been part of a particular tradition in the past doesn't mean we can't embrace that tradition right now. All traditions began somewhere.

I'm trying to start a new tradition with out-of-town friends: each month, I try to write somebody and call somebody I normally wouldn't write or call. It seems like such an insignificant gesture, and yet I know it won't get done if I don't make a commitment to doing it and trying to make it a tradition.

Finally, our faith journeys probably have included periods of doubt, rebellion, and apathy. And yet the essence of faith is leaving the past, living beyond the feelings and having the courage to believe our Creator's promises. Our culture is continually offering trendy, short-term solutions to life's dilemmas. What we really need is long-term trust in the traditions of God.

Pilgrimage to the Past

❧

In the background of the long-distance call last Thanksgiving, I could hear the voices of my family. One of my sister's twins was laughing. My father was taking orders for sandwiches. And, in the distance, 88-year-old Grandpa Schu was talking—what else?—fresh produce.

In a few minutes, the phone call came to an end. "Happy Thanksgiving," my mother said. "We miss you."

I said goodbye. And the line went dead.

Never is the tug of home as strong as when you hang up following a holiday phone call. What is it about this magnetic force of family?

I'm reminded of it now because at Thanksgiving and Christmas, it pulls stronger than at any other time of the year. It's not that way for everybody, I know. Some find their strongest bonds in friends, not family; for others, looking back is simply too painful.

But some of us find ourselves in a paradoxical pattern: Physically, we grow up and leave home; emotionally, we grow up and never leave home.

We brashly march off to college, smug in our newfound independence. Two weeks later, we're sitting in a closet-size dorm room, counting the days until Thanksgiving as our stomachs do battle with cafeteria food.

We graduate and hitch our U-Hauls to a star, following jobs wherever they might lead. But we come back every time we unpack the handed-down Christmas tree ornaments or see a home-state license plate.

We establish traditions at a home of our own. But while worthy in themselves, they are offsprings of something deeper—reasonable facsimiles, but not yet the real thing. Like an astronaut's view of earth, the past gets more intriguing the farther away you get.

So, if possible, we return, and probably not as simply as traveling over the river and through the woods. The fact is, regardless of where we live, most of us are from somewhere else, often somewhere else far away.

Many of us are refugees who came to a place for the future but are inextricably linked to the past. It doesn't matter whether it's California or Connecticut, the homeland pulls.

It's a subtle, unseen pull like the moon tugging the tides. And just as the ebbs and flows of oceans become cycles of coming and going, so do our lives. Each day, in our routine reading of the newspaper, we check the temperature back home. We imagine what, say, 32 degrees would be like there in November. How it would feel.

Each change of season, we picture what it would look like back home. And, if possible, each holiday season we get the neighbors to feed the cats, and we return. Whether we fly or drive, take a train or a snowmobile, the journey is the same: a pilgrimage to our past.

When we return, we're sometimes reminded less of how the place has changed than how *we* have changed—some for the better, some for the worse. Scrapbooks bring back the good memories; trips home bring back them all.

But it's good to remember. Not to mire ourselves in the past, but to learn from it, to use it as a reference point. When we look at the dismantled stage, we sometimes discover that while making the journey from childhood to adulthood, we discarded some things we shouldn't have. And brought along some things we should have discarded.

If the past has been painful, we search the prickly vine for the edible berries.

We dust off treasured traditions, such as the three-generation street football game, followed immediately by mass moaning and groaning from two of the three generations.

We renew relationships, or at least search for a smidgeon of common ground with the cousin-in-law we haven't seen in five years.

We honor the heritage of family that time and distance have diluted but not destroyed.

Home, you see, is a place for belonging, a place for acceptance, a place where everybody knows your name.

Home is people who remember the time your uncle, the Santa Claus, brought you a year's supply of Spearmint gum, and you—at age two—broke into tears. It's the inexplicable security of knowing your mother's homemade candy will always taste the same.

Home is not an airbrushed haven manufactured by Hallmark. Sometimes babies cry, children pout, adults disagree. Sometimes there's an empty chair at the dinner table, a subtle reminder of death or divorce.

But if we care enough about this collection of kin, such things can be overcome. And if we look hard enough, we can see the calm amid the confusion. Far removed from the storm of sugar-fueled children, your mother is quietly reading your youngest son a bedtime story.

And so we return to our roots. If we can't, we call. But it's never the same. It's not the same as smelling the bayberry and fiberglass, that holiday blend known only to families whose fathers build sailboats in the garage. And it's not the same as shooting a few baskets on the hoop that once seemed so tall.

To return means experiencing that strange feeling of being both visitor and resident, as if we are absentee owners holding titles to property of the past.

On one hand, we know this place will never again be home. On the other hand, we know it will always be home.

The Joy of Camping

❧

*T*he clouds above Suttle Lake in Oregon's Cascade Mountains were thick and black, like the smoke from burning tires. When you're 10 years old and think camping is the greatest thing since the invention of Fizzies, you don't want to see a sky like that, particularly on the day your family vacation has begun.

So you wait and you listen and you hope and then you hear them: those reassuring words from your father.

"Ah, it's just a squall," he said, looking at the charcoal sky. "It'll pass in no time."

My guess is it passed sometime shortly before my high school graduation. Our family—Mom, Dad and my older sister—spent that entire weekend sitting under a tarp, listening to the rain fill the plastic and spill to the ground. We told every knock-knock joke we'd ever heard. We not only read every article in the two dogeared *Reader's Digests* we had brought, but the magazine's staff box and Statement of Ownership as well. Twice.

And wouldn't have traded the memory for anything.

I thought about that vacation not long ago while camping with my wife and two boys, the oldest of whom is now 10. I was thinking about how some families are linked by a recreational pursuit passed down from generation to generation. And how, for our family, that pursuit is camping. Like my parents before me and my father's parents before him, we are woven together by some inexplicable desire to get smoke in our eyes, sit on fishing lures and offer ourselves as human sacrifices to tribes of bloodthirsty mosquitoes.

Why? It's easy to answer that question when you're watching a full moon reflect on a high-mountain lake or observing a chipmunk steal M&Ms or reading Psalms as the wind tickles the branches of the Douglas Firs. It's tougher to answer when it's 5 A.M. and you're the only one in the tent not asleep, a tree root poking between your shoulder blades and some guy snoring three camps away like a chain saw with a busted carburetor.

When my oldest son was four years old, we had been fishing for days in a small boat when he suddenly said, "Dad, why do we fish?"

He was not concerned about the ethics of the sport. He was perplexed because he had never seen me catch a fish and didn't understand the object of our mission. You sat in a boat the size of a bathtub and threw worms over the side and whispered while your cramped legs went to sleep. What sort of strange ritual was this?

Now, as an adult, I find myself pondering the same question. What sort of strange ritual is this? A father and son fishing. A family camping. Why give up microwave ovens and soft mattresses for 8-foot boats and outhouses that are too far away when you need one and too close when you don't?

Part of the reason we camp and fish, I think, is because of that heartfelt utterance of Tevye in "Fiddler on the Roof:" *Tradition!* Ours is a world where traditions are easily trampled. So as parents, we want our children to have the experiences we had as a child.

Thus, we go camping—and bring the flashlight whose batteries have been dead since the Carter Administration. We forget the can opener and so mutilate a can of beef chili stew with a knife. And we use nearly as much blood, sweat and tears putting up a 12-foot nylon tent as the Egyptians used building the pyramids. Why? *Tradition!*

Take camp songs. As a boy, I remember groaning as my mother broke into songs while we sat around the fire, including one about how we "love to go a wandering . . ." Now, I'm the one who breaks into camp songs as my children moan in sweet harmony. Why? *Tradition!*

Take marshmallows. They make no particular sense. They're full of sugar. They usually become charred torches with the epicurean appeal of coal. And the mushy part inside usually winds up in a child's hair, attracts a weekend's worth of pine needles and ultimately has to be clear-cut with a pair of scissors. But you must roast marshmallows while camping. Why? *Tradition!*

Why else do we camp? Because it brings us face to face, not only as tent sardines but as human beings. At home, too often we gather around the TV, each of us reacting to it, not to each other. High in the mountains, we gather around a fire, which draws us to each other and not to itself.

Never mind that the same fire, before the weekend is out, will melt the toe of at least one son's tennis shoes and spew ashes into someone's hot chocolate. It will also stir memories, prompt small talk and, as the evening deepens and the embers glow more faintly, gently nudge us into Big Talk.

Amid a world in technological overdrive, camping brings us back to the basics. At home, our imaginations are nearly rendered useless by computers and gadgets and gizmos. In the woods, we're forced to use our creativity. To improvise. To work together as a team. To figure out how to get Mom's sunglasses off the bottom of the lake, 12 feet down.

We learn things while camping—not only how to whittle a hot-dog stick but, say, what it means to be honest. Once, while fishing with my father, people in nearby boats had caught their legal limits but continued to catch more. When my father and I reached our limit he started the motor (16th pull) and we headed for shore. Though such things may seem insignificant at the time, sons remember them.

I remember the time my father let me drive our boat alone across a lake for the first time; a rite of passage from boyhood to manhood.

I remember the time we were asleep in the tent when our dog Jet started barking wildly, bothered by something in our camp. My mother was sure it was a bear. In fact, it was my father's underwear, hanging on a clothesline, eerily silhouetted in the light of a full moon.

As we grow from children to adults, we tuck such memories away and forget them, like photographs stowed in an attic. But every now and then, we remember the feel of piercing the cool water with a swan dive, the smell of bacon and eggs on a grill, the sound of an ax splitting the evening's firewood. And we try to allow our children to feel and smell and hear those same things.

It isn't important that we have the perfect experience while camping. Or that we're super campers whose boat motors always start on the first pull and whose air mattresses never go flat in the night. What matters is that we spend time communicating with each other, communicating with God and enjoying this amazing creation of His.

What's important is simply being together, as my family was two years ago at a campground called Denny Creek. The thunder sounded as if we were sitting beneath a celestial bowling alley and the rain was pelting our tent. My sons looked at me, seeking reassurance. What I told them marked yet another rite of passage for me, not from boy to man, but from son to father.

"Ah, it's just a squall," I said. "It'll pass in no time."

CHAPTER FOUR

Trading Technology for Talk

I t is the simplest of cartoons: A young man and woman are standing alone on an ocean shore. The woman has on a set of earphones while the man appears to have just taken his off. "Wow!" he says. "When you take off your earphones, you can hear the roar of the surf!"

Whether we acknowledge it or not, the surf has been roaring since Day Three of creation. But we've become so dependent on technology that we don't hear the sound of it. As with most cartoons, what makes us laugh at this one is that, for all its oversimplification and humor, it contains a profound truth. Technology has become the double-edged sword of the late 20th century. While enabling us to live more comfortably, it also entices us to block out the goodness of the world. It is easy to become deaf to the sound of the surf, to the leading of God, to the concerns of others.

The pervasiveness of technology also causes us to overlook its influence as a distraction. Have you ever been in an office when the power suddenly went out? Until then, you had never realized how noisy the computers, typewriters, lights and ventilation system were—and how wonderfully peaceful it was without them.

Television delivers an average of 29 channels to each U.S. household. Rented movies plugged into a VCR have become our dominant form of entertainment. Video games and home computers aren't far behind; based on sales, more than one in four U.S. households has a Nintendo video game system.

You needn't be against technology to be concerned about the influence of technology. Frankly, I like being able to fix microwave popcorn in three minutes, write stories on a word processor and videotape busy vacations so I can come home and find out if I had a good time. But I'm also concerned that a preoccupation with technology can diminish our interaction with God and with people around us. That instead of complementing the more significant parts of our lives, technology *can replace* the more significant parts of our lives. And that, left unchecked, it can essentially *become* our lives.

The average home now has a television or radio on 11 hours a day.[1] Is it any wonder that some adults—even some well-educated adults—express highs and lows depending on how their favorite television characters fare? Ever find yourself forgetting a Bible memory verse but flawlessly singing the McDonald's commercial?

We have become almost obsessed with communication. We have portable phones in the house, mobile phones outside the house, beepers, recorded messages and call-waiting. With modems, we can now communicate with each other via computers. Using fax machines, we can exchange printed information almost instantaneously. And, thanks to satellite dishes, a rancher in Wyoming can get as many channels as the stockbroker in New York.

But for all that, what do counselors say is the major problem in interpersonal relationships? Communication. A woman who operates a home for runaway boys was telling me about the teenagers from middle- and upper-class families who wind up on the streets. "What amazes me most about parents," she said, "is that they can be so full of love for a child and not be able to let the child know it."

Often ballyhooed as a byte-size savior, the computer has transformed the business world. Marketers use them to pinpoint people who will buy their products. In the fall of 1990, Microsoft introduced computer software that can transfer handwriting into print. A few months later, Hitachi Ltd. introduced a computer that mimics the learning and problem-solving capabilities of the human brain, able to carry out 2.3 billion operations *per second*.

But for all that, the Information Age is not saving America. Able to access reams of good information, we nevertheless make poor choices. If information is a savior, why, after decades of information about the clear dangers of smoking, do people continue to smoke? Why, after decades of increased educational information, have the average scores for SAT tests dropped the last five years in a row, the Class of '91's the poorest in the history of the test? Why, after the glut of self-help books, is the American divorce rate still the highest in the world?

"It takes hard work, sustained effort, sacrifice and compromise to make a relationship a good one," wrote sociologist William A. Donohue. "These are values that in our material world have been made obsolete. But they are just as necessary today as ever before when it comes to social relationships. We may be modern in terms of our technological achievements and standard of living, but we are no different from the ancients in terms of human needs."[2]

Despite a dizzying array of electronic entertainment choices, many teenagers find none that satisfies their thirst for fun and adventure. Interviewing teenagers with wild punk hair styles, I asked why they would spike their hair with Elmer's Glue, dye it turquoise or shave it off completely. "Boredom," they said.

Technology can bring us closer together, but it also pulls us apart. Many teenagers' rooms resemble miniature home electronics stores. Headphones make it possible for two walkers to pass each other without exchanging a word.

A university sociologist was telling me about a visitor to the U.S. from the Philippines. In the evenings, the woman would go outside, as she did back home, to mingle with people. But the neighborhoods were vacant; everyone was inside watching TV. "What do people do here?" she asked. "The people seem so lonely."

Television rarely draws families closer together. Occasionally, programs are valuable learning tools. Some are simply good entertainment. And some actually provoke valuable family discussions. But, for the most part, television provides a good excuse *not* to interact with those around us.

What's compounded the problem is that television has not become just another ingredient in the leisure-time mixture. It has become the main course. In 1965, television comprised 30 percent of our spare time, by far more than anything else; by 1985, it had risen to 38 percent.[3]

Rather than getting involved in life, we have become content to experience life secondhand. A few years after Mount St. Helens erupted, a group of people were inside a visitors center watching a videotape of the first eruption. Suddenly, outside, the mountain began belching ash. A ranger rushed inside to tell the people that they could see the real thing by walking about 15 feet. Nobody moved.

In a sense, we're becoming a nation of spectators rather than risk takers. Why risk starting a friendship with a neighbor when I can vicariously experience relationships on TV? Why take a walk with my children when they're so absorbed in Nintendo? Why discover God's creation for myself when I can rent the video?

If people have unrealistic expectations of life, one reason is because TV has provided an unrealistic approach to problem-solving. Even commercials suggest instant changes are possible, providing you buy the right product.

The result? We expect the same simplistic solutions in relationships, then are shocked to find there's no such thing as solid-state marriages, push-button children and ready-to-use friends.

Although we've allowed technology to use us as much as we use it, some people are realizing that it's no replacement for the real thing. I know of a family who stuffed their television in a closet when they had trouble communicating. Other families camp on their vacations so they can focus on each other without having to worry about the ring of the phone. Still others resist the Nintendo pull—and their children do not hold hunger strikes to protest.

It's time to bring back the human touch to our relationships, time to replace technology with talk, time to gather around the kitchen table instead of leaving messages on the family answering machine.

Human interaction used to come naturally, but because of technological distractions, we now must make it happen. Interacting with each other means making some simple decisions about things such as how much TV we watch and how often the kids can have headphones on.

From time to time, we need to pull the plug on technology and listen to life. Pick blackberries. Watch it snow. Lay on the grass and look at clouds. Write a letter to a friend who only expects one at Christmas. Look at the words in a hymn. Thumb through a photo album. Notice the expression on our children's face as they draw a picture. Write a poem for our spouse.

Amid the "noise" of technology, we need to listen to each other—really listen. I'll sometimes find myself nodding and saying "uh-huh" to people but not really listening to what's being said. And I wonder: How many times have I done the same to God, rushing through my morning quiet time as if it were a mandatory assignment instead of a freewill privilege?

We serve a God who is concerned with the little moments of our lives, who cares for the sparrow and yet cares for us more, who would drop all to save one lost sheep. In that spirit, we, too, should care about the details of life, pursuing each day with passion, connecting with those around us with a subtle sense of urgency.

In Thornton Wilder's "Our Town," Emily, who died while giving birth to her second child, is given a chance to witness the day she turned 12. In doing so, she realizes all the nuances of life she had never seen. "It goes so fast. We don't have time to look at one another," she says. "Good-by world.... Good-by to clocks ticking... and Mama's sunflowers. And food and coffee. And new-ironed dresses and hot baths... and sleeping and waking up.... Do any human beings ever realize life while they live it—every, every minute?"[4]

With headphones on, you cannot hear the sound of clocks ticking, the small voices of people in need, the concerns of those we love and the whisper of the God we serve. Day after day, week after week, the surf crashes magnificently to the shores of our lives.

Isn't it time we stopped and listened to it?

A Place to Be Still

ॐ

I was in British Columbia recently when I noticed something odd about the houses. At first, I couldn't figure out what it was. Then it dawned on me.

They had front porches.

Remember porches?

They're like soda shops, one of those good things that faded away without most of us noticing. Older neighborhoods still have them. So do a few new developments. But porches—large, bona fide, sit-in-a-rocking-chair porches—are rare these days.

And that says something about life in America, circa 1992. Our grandparents and parents grew up in a world full of porches. At the end of a summer day, the folks sat on the porch and watched the world go by. It was a place to catch up on who was doing what in the neighborhood. A place to think. It was a place to read the evening paper, to talk, to smell a summer breeze and sip lemonade and listen to distant dogs barking and pint-sized baseball players arguing about close calls at home.

My wife's grandfather, a farmer, made special chairs out of old tractor seats so he and his wife could sit on their porch, smell the wheat fields, listen to the crickets and look at the stars above Oregon's Coast Range.

In the '50s, suburbia arrived. Traffic increased. A friend of mine fortunate to have a wonderful front porch says he and his wife never sit on it anymore. "Too noisy," he says.

More than anything else, today's lack of front porches is metaphorical, a symbol of an inward-oriented culture that contradicts God's call to be outward-oriented people.

In the last 30 years, we've become a more private society. We've retreated to the backyard, building patios and decks and hot tubs. We've built fences to separate us from neighbors. We've even developed members-only neighborhoods with gates and guards and magnetic cards.

A friend who recently moved into a new suburban neighborhood noticed how seldom he sees his neighbors. In the morning, the automatic garage-door openers click into gear and people leave for work; in the evening, the automatic garage-doors click back into gear and people come home from work. But nobody is ever *seen*. Our homes have become hermetically sealed from the rest of the world—airtight architectural Baggies in which nothing touches us.

A sociology professor was telling me how teenagers are caught in a sort of no-man's land. Once, a teenager was not only accountable to his parents but, to a lesser extent, his neighbors. Now, his parents are too busy for him and he doesn't even know his neighbors, much less feel any sense of obligation to them.

Television, not the peace of a front porch, has become our post-dinner magnet. Once, a couple might have spent an evening talking or watching the sky shift from blue to peach to black. After TV arrived, they spent their evenings watching *Dragnet* and *Mr. Ed*.

The average middle-aged American watches 30 hours of television a week, meaning a lot of sunsets don't get seen and a lot of words don't get spoken.

With television, we could suddenly be entertained and informed by people clear across the world. Who needed the Smiths next door, when we could watch *Lives of the Rich and Famous* from Paris? Who needed to watch the kids play hide-and-seek when we could watch *The Brady Bunch*?

In the last decade, video has pulled us further from the outside world. We spend our summer evenings sitting in front of entertainment centers, not on porches.

In a sense, porches are everything the '90s aren't. This is a high-tech decade; porches are simple. This is a fast-paced decade; porches require time. This is an action decade; porches don't do a thing.

Porches accompanied more innocent times, when young lovers held hands on them and when George and Mary embraced in *It's a Wonderful Life* and the T-shirted neighbor yelled from his own front porch, "Why don't you kiss her instead of talking her to death?"

And yet what porches represent—a place to be still and examine ourselves and the world around us—seems to be a need that abides, despite the differences in the decades.

In a world where it's easy to get wrapped up in technology, in the nonstop striving to do it all, in madly crossing off the to-do lists, something has gotten lost. Something important. Phones are ringing and beepers are beeping and people are dashing from here to there.

But we could still benefit from having a place where we can talk, a place to think. A place to read, talk, smell a summer breeze, sip lemonade and listen to distant dogs barking and pint-sized baseball players arguing about close calls at home.

Beyond Electricity

ᏋᎧ

*M*ost of us have a Christmas present that stands above the rest, one that comes to mind every December when we smell the pitch of an evergreen and hear the sound of carols. For me, it is an electric football game.

After months of anticipation, I found it under the tree as an eight-year-old, one of those priceless dreams that lists for $12.95.

For those unfamiliar with electric football, it is played by 22 one-inch-high players who are motivated not by a fiery coach or a six-digit contract, but by good vibrations. You line the plastic players up, flip a switch and they vibrate their way around the metal field in a frenzy, as if the team prankster had put Deep Heat in their jockstraps as a joke.

I played the game hour after hour, setting up plays and flipping the switch. *Bzzzzzzzzz.* Set up. *Bzzzzzzzzz.* Set up. *Bzzzzzzzzz.*

Alas, like most Christmas presents, this one broke before Groundhog's Day. I was crushed, my mother secretly elated. "That thing," she told me a few years ago, "sounded like a high-speed drill."

For me, life was suddenly empty. But out of the hollowness came hope. One day, I took half the plastic players in one hand, half in the other hand

and smashed them together, almost out of frustration. Then it dawned on me: Who needed electricity?

I designated a ball carrier and a defense and smashed them together. Why, of course! I could improvise. I created my own games. In my best nasal voice, I became the game's play-by-play announcer. I stacked books around the field to simulate grandstands. I used a desk lamp to play night-games "under the lights."

Still, I needed more realism. With color crayons, I shaded the end zones to simulate the end-zone designs at the stadium where my favorite college team played. My mother, thrilled that I had created *bzzzzz*-less fun, contributed a record album with college fight songs that I used to create pre-game excitement. My father made a set of coat-hanger goal posts that were much classier than the ones that came with the game.

That's not all. Given that these were the days before domed stadiums and artificial turf, I needed some grime. So I brought in mud from Mom's garden. And the ultimate touch, reserved for only special occasions, was snow, though the unimaginative may have recognized it as Ivory Soap flakes.

With all these additions, an amazing transformation had taken place. The game no longer ran on electricity, but something much more powerful. It ran on imagination. For years, I continued to play it, even as my collection of players diminished from 22 to five, some of whom were missing body parts. (But what a five they were; even my headless middle linebacker made All-American.)

Such imagination is an endangered species with children these days. Oh, it's still available, but too many parents are unwilling to let their children try their's out—and too willing to let technology fill the void.

We buy our children video games with built-in imagination. We let them sit in front of television sets watching programs created by someone else's imagination. And we buy them expensive toys nearly devoid of imagination. But what do we do to foster our child's *own* imagination?

Some contend that children today have been exposed to so many fascinating things—say, Disneyland rides that make you feel you're in outer space—that kids are desensitized to fascination.

But the real problem is that they've been under-exposed to the wonders of imagination. The clues come early that children love to imagine. What does the four-year-old do on Christmas Eve? Tears into a present, tosses it aside and spends the rest of the evening playing with the box. What does the child do who's just watched a detective cartoon? Plays detective.

But with an assist from Madison Avenue, we've come to believe that fun is something you buy, not something you create. We've become dependent on someone else to tell our children how to have fun— the makers of video games, the creators of one-dimensional toys, the writers of 101-things-to-do books.

It's simpler to pop in a video than help your children create their own rendition of *The Man from Snowy River*. Easier to let McDonald's take care of a child's birthday party than to create a party of your own. But what's more fun—and beneficial—for the child?

Perhaps what we as parents need to do is allow our children to think for themselves. If a toy breaks—not exactly uncommon in our mass-produced world—perhaps we should encourage our child to make-do rather than rushing to the store to replace it.

When given a chance to use their imaginations, kids respond with enthusiasm. What eight-year-old can't have fun with a box of mill ends? Can't create something from a half dozen wrapping-paper tubes? Won't build a dam with the water that drains down the driveway while you're washing the car?

Sure, there's a price to pay. Allow the kids to pretend your backyard is Yankee Stadium and you might wind up with base paths worn into the lawn; you also might wind up with kids happily lost in big-league dreams.

Give a child 300 obsolete business cards from work and you may, indeed, find business cards in nooks and crannies of the house for the next 10 years; you also might find kids playing bank or using them to write Scripture memorization.

Encourage a child to read, and you might wind up spending a little more money each month on books; you also might wind up spending less time on TV patrol.

I'm convinced that a broken electric football game led to my becoming a writer. Once my make-believe games were over, I would write a newspaper story, complete with hand-drawn "photographs."

At 14, I was writing Little League stories for the local paper and have been in the business ever since.

Mom saved the electric football set for me. Rusted and creased, it hangs downstairs in my workshop where a glance at it still triggers memories and provokes a question that has lingered for the past 30 years: Namely, whatever happened to those 17 players who disappeared?

Some say they were disgruntled with their contracts and left to play for a better owner. Others say they got tired of having to labor in mud and Ivory soap flakes.

As for me, I suspect a more gruesome reason for their sudden disappearance: My mother's vacuum cleaner.

CHAPTER FIVE

Trading Self-Centeredness for Self-Sacrifice

It's a blustery fall day, the cranky skies spitting occasional raindrops as if to signal worse things to come. But on a residential street, the woman's flower stand is open as usual, offering the world a smidgen of sunshine. Seven days a week, 52 weeks a year, her home-grown flowers sit on the tattered card table outside her house. Chrysanthemums, zinnias, baby's breath and more, all bunched in coffee cans. Two bucks a bundle. Just leave your money on the table—or put it in the fishing creel on the porch. A little short this week? Take the flowers. At 86, the woman who toils in the garden to produce them isn't out to get rich, just pay for her fertilizer and perhaps a few root-beer floats for her grandsons.

She is from a different generation. In her simplicity and selflessness, she represents the flip side to the Now Generation, whose fulfillment is often found in elevation of one's self. In her daily routine from garden to card table, it's as if she were caught in some sort of time warp, blindly settling for so little when there was so much more she could have.

Didn't she understand that she could have maximized her profits by selling bulk to a retailer? That, with a computer and the right software package, she could have streamlined her operation, boosting her net intake?

No she did not, nor did she want to. What she understood was this: "The people who buy my flowers are happy—and that makes me happy." She wasn't out for herself. She was out for others. A strange concept, indeed, in a time when our culture relentlessly beckons us to exalt ourselves.

For baby boomers, it wasn't supposed to be this way. Remember, this was the generation inspired by President John F. Kennedy, whose death is apparently seared into a generation's collective memory more deeply than his life. "Ask not what your country can do for you," he exhorted, "but what you can do for your country." The call exhorted people to sacrifice, to put the collective good above self. True, some have done exactly that—for example, soldiers who served in the Persian Gulf and Vietnam, and civilians who served in the Peace Corps. But more have asked what their country could do for them. What their spouse could do for them. What their friends could do for them. What their church could do for them. And what God could do for them.

In the '70s, self-gratification became the goal for many. A Rutgers University poll showed that while only 41 percent of the public at large felt doing the things that offer personal satisfaction and pleasure were more important than working hard and doing what is expected, 67 percent of baby boomers felt that way.[1]

After a decade of searching for self in the '80s, boomers tried to find their identity in work. A large segment of baby boomers embraced the 9-to-5 world with vigor. On the outside, it looked like a nose-to-grindstone, duty-bound work ethic. But at its core was ego. The ultimate goal was not some selfless attempt to put bread on the table or to loyally serve the company, but to get ahead. To climb higher. To be recognized. For women, in particular, to become something other than a homemaker.

Meanwhile, boomers discovered bicycles and wind surfing and rowing machines and a bunch of gadgets that nobody knew existed one day but couldn't live without the next. Fulfillment, it seemed, was only a catalog-order away. Alas, like using a credit card, the ease of acquisition ultimately asks a price—and relationships have paid that price. Why? Because though Madison Avenue and Hollywood want us to believe that relationships are fueled by spontaneous sensual combustion—the pleasure principle—they are in fact fueled by consistent commitment— the work ethic. Not self-absorption but self-sacrifice.

Good families require submission of the individual to the collective interests of the others. Many are not prepared to bear such a thing. In a have-it-all world, the idea of self-denial seems backward.

For example, while some women work outside the home because they enjoy it or because it's a financial necessity, many others do so because the workplace has supplanted home as a validation of their worth. There is prestige for those who work outside the home while there is near-pity for those who stay home—as if there were something intrinsically significant in punching letters into a word processor and something intrinsically insignificant in being the most important person in the development of a child. In only one decade, our values have done a U-turn.

Our culture has decided that humbling jobs such as motherhood are nowhere jobs. And yet humility—giving ourselves selflessly to others—is a cornerstone of the Christian faith. "Do nothing out of selfish ambition or vain conceit, but in humility consider others better than yourselves," Paul wrote. "Each of you should look not only to your own interests, but also to the interests of others" (Philippians 2:3-4).

He did not say we should consider ourselves door-mats, but to consider the needs of others. Whether the relationship is between husband and wife, parent and child, worker and co-worker, friend and friend, elder and elder, humility must be a priority. And Christians who smugly believe we're "above that" are ignoring the obvious.

Last year our church's pastor was speaking on the topic of church leaders and their need to serve God and others. At the exact time, we later learned through the newspaper, an argument broke out in an elder meeting in an evangelical church across the country and an elder was shot and wounded. How can we expect to impact the world for Christ if we cannot even find peace with each other?

In a me-oriented world we follow an other-oriented God. "Nobody should seek his own good, but the good of others," wrote Paul (1 Corinthians 10:24). We're called to follow not our own desires, but the desires of God. "The way of a fool seems right to him, but a wise man listens to advice" (Proverbs 12:15). We're called to help those in need. "If anyone has material possession and sees his brother in need but has no pity on him, how can the love of God be in him?" (1 John 3:17).

If each of us takes care of himself, as our me-first culture suggests, the maximum number of people who can benefit is one. But if we reach out to others, the number is limitless.

We tend to remember times when people have reached out to us. Selfless acts linger as sweet memories. Early in our marriage, my wife and I heated our house totally with a wood stove, with wood we cut ourselves. But one particular fall, our pickup broke down and, with winter breathing down our necks, we sat at the dinner table one evening, worried about what we were going to do. Suddenly, we heard something on the side of our house. Going outside, we found friends from our church—a retired couple both in their late 60s—sitting in their pickup truck with a cord of fresh-cut pine in the back.

"Where can we stack it?" the man asked.

Other people's sacrifices inspire me. I think of a woman who, though one of the finest teachers in her district, put her career on hold to be at home with her children. Of a man who loved to kayak but gave it up to become the scout leader of his son's troop. Of doctors I know who, each year, give up thousands of dollars and weeks of time with their families so they can give medical care to impoverished people in Haiti. Of a group of parents who, when their church's youth pastor left and no interim pastor was appointed, made a commitment to run the high school group themselves.

I think of a man who was head of a large department store but gave it up to go to seminary and become a pastor. Of a couple whose marriage hit the rocks, but instead of abandoning ship, made repairs and sailed onto smoother waters. Of a newly married man who, after some difficulty in the relationship, went to a marriage conference and faced his own shortcomings rather than berating his wife for hers.

The common denominator among these people? God and other people—not self and possessions—were their life's priorities. All were willing to take a cut in pay, pride and prestige. As Oswald Chambers wrote: "It is in the sphere of humiliation that we find our true worth to God, that is where our faithfulness is revealed."[2]

Recently, following a college football game, I watched as fans of the winning team swarmed onto the field. Then something strange happened. As the crowd surged past him, one of the players from the losing team worked his way through this jubilant sea of humanity; no easy task, but he was intent on getting somewhere. I wondered where. Finally, he came up to a player from the winning team, shook his hand and said, "You played a great game." He had humbled himself, gone against the grain and done something that a lot of folks would never have considered.

It was the type of small sacrifice to which we must each dedicate ourselves daily—not grabbing for ourselves, but reaching out for others, even if it's not easy.

"For whoever exalts himself will be humbled, and whoever humbles himself will be exalted," said Jesus (Matthew 23:12).

When hearing these words, I think back to the woman who diligently worked her flower beds to brighten the days of other people. She knew the secret that almost seems lost on a generation where self-sacrifice is blurred by self-centeredness. In giving to others, she was the one who received. In a world where so many are blinded by self, she was the one who saw so very clearly.

A Cup of Cold Water

ॐ

It is early evening. The woman has been in labor for days but the baby will not budge. The mother's pelvis is too small.

In most parts of the United States, a simple Caesarean section would be performed at a hospital and everyone would live happily ever after. But this is not the United States.

This is Savane Carree, Haiti, a remote mountain community with no hospital, no doctor and no electricity. This is the most impoverished country in the Western Hemisphere, a place where living comes hard and dying comes easy. One in four children won't make it past age five.

For the American doctor, the choices are clear. If the woman is driven to a hospital in Dessalines, where he could safely perform a C-section, there is at least a chance. If not, the mother and baby will likely die. But separating Savane Carree from the hospital are three hours worth of mud, potholes and a river that must be crossed through—not over—seven times. At night.

Miss Maxine, a 59-year-old missionary, says the medical team has no choice. She hops behind the steering wheel and they're off. I watch as the jeep, an IV fastened to its ceiling hand strap with twine, bounces down the road and vanishes into the darkness.

The scene is seared into my mind—like so many other scenes after spending two weeks in this Third World country. I went to serve on a medical team from Washington state, coming home astounded at the needs in this world and amazed at the people willing to help meet those needs.

At 5 A.M., members of the Haiti Medical Team, sponsored by Yakima Free Methodist church of Yakima, Wash., begin emerging from their gumdrop tents to begin a typical day. The Haitians, meanwhile, have already begun crowding to the front of the cinder-block church that will be converted into a clinic.

Most of the people have never seen a doctor and have walked or ridden donkeys miles to do so, winding their way on trails and roads from their thatch-roofed huts.

As word spreads of the clinic, the crowds begin arriving earlier and earlier each day. One night I hear some noises in a dirt-floor schoolhouse next to the church. Shining my flashlight inside, I see dozens of sleeping Haitians, wall-to-wall, waiting for morning and a chance to see a doctor or dentist.

During the two-week clinic, the team sees more than 2,000 patients. They dispense drugs, pull teeth, cleanse wounds, do minor surgery. They see it all: dehydrated children with only weeks to live. Tumors the size of tennis balls. Infected belly buttons caused by cutting the umbilical cord with a tin can lid. Malnutrition. Worms. And more.

Amid such obstacles, team members wear buttons touting the team motto: "No problem." The message? With God on our side, anything can be overcome—even a broken generator and a team-record 10 flat tires.

Improvisation and duct tape help us survive. The side of a cardboard box becomes a splint. A chalkboard is turned over to become a pharmacy table. A plastic tarp is hung in the corner of the church to create an intensive care unit. We even improvise with our skills: A software engineer assists a dentist. A patent attorney fixes a major leak in Savane Carree's water line. A homemaker helps an elderly woman take a pill. A college student scrubs a child's diseased skin.

One night, a sudden rain shower forces the team into the church to eat dinner. The worship service will begin in half an hour, and a few dozen Haitians have already arrived, seated on wooden benches. They quietly watch us eat as we try to ignore the unavoidable clash of haves and have-nots. Finally, the team begins sharing its food and cups of fruit drinks.

The Haitians, mostly children, gratefully accept. It is the gospel at its grassroots best—Matthew 10:42 with a raspberry twist. "And if anyone gives a cup of cold water to one of these little ones because he is my disciple, I tell you the truth, he will certainly not lose his reward."

Quiet heroics abound. After seeing nearly 100 patients that day, one doctor doggedly patches up the victims of a bus crash. Once finished, he wastes no time setting up the pews and microphone system for the evening church service. After a quick bite to eat, he returns to find a Haitian woman in the congregation hemorrhaging. With the help of a nurse, he calmly takes the woman into the ICU unit, stops the bleeding and returns to sing Haitian praise hymns.

No problem.

As clinic continues, the doctors do what they can. Sometimes, nothing can be done. Working in the pharmacy one day, I'm handed a prescription card from a nurse. It prescribes only one thing: "Prayer."

Other times, the doctors save a life that probably would have been lost. A year before the November 1988 team arrived, a boy was brought to the clinic with severe burns from a fire intended to ward off evil spirits. The previous medical team had treated him and rushed him to a hospital. Now, he's back to visit—and he's healthy.

Three years earlier, tiny "Wizzy" was brought to the clinic on the verge of starvation. She was 19 months old and weighed only eight pounds—"a sack of bones," according to one doctor. Now, she's healthy, strong and beautiful. Her mother shows up at the clinic with a basket of fresh eggs to say thank you.

As our stay nears its end, the crowds grow larger. People try to bribe the guards with what little money they have. They pass babies through the iron bars to friends inside. So many push against the gates that the hinges on the iron door break—not because the crowd is unruly but because of its collective force.

It's hard to feel malice toward them; they only want to live, to overcome the pain that's gone on so long—like the woman in labor who left in the jeep, her hand clutching the hand of a U.S. nurse who had voluntarily been with her since early that morning.

A week earlier, the nurse had been living safe in a cocoon of American comfort, a place where some see hardship as having to change TV channels by hand instead of remote control. Now, as the jeep bounces toward Dessalines, she holds the Haitian woman's hand and wipes the sweat from the woman's face as if the two were sisters. Black and white, rich and poor, young and old—the differences between the two women fade as the darkness deepens.

Miss Maxine, the missionary driving the jeep, makes the usual three-hour trip to the hospital in two. The doctor works fast; at midnight—minutes away—the generator will kick off and he'll have to do his C-section by flashlight. He performs the surgery in 11 minutes.

In the sticky warmth of the Haitian night, a cry of hope interrupts, if only for a moment, this country's day-to-day despair.

It's a boy.

A 20th-Century Good Samaritan

*F*inished with work at his father's market, a boy named Tommy prepared to head home on his bike. Dusk had set in. Traffic was thick on Oregon's Highway 99E. A light rain was falling. But Tommy knew the seven miles of highway like the feel of his own bike; he had ridden the stretch day in and day out for two years.

He kissed his stepmother goodbye and hopped on his bike. "Be careful," she reminded him.

Meanwhile, a man from Washington state was at a nearby Burger King, changing out of his work clothes. After supervising the repair of an industrial freezer system, he was driving a rental car back to Portland International Airport. The freezer system had been fixed. He would soon be reunited with his wife and two-year-old daughter. All was well with the world. He headed north on Highway 99E.

Moments later, he saw it in the car's headlights: a bicycle on its side, just off the road. It didn't seem right, not on a rainy November night like this. Not so close to the highway.

He quickly pulled the car to the shoulder and ran back toward the bicycle, some 60 yards away. That's when he spotted Tommy. He was on his side, with his face buried in gravel. A pool of blood had formed around his head.

His jean jacket had foot-long rips in it and his upper body was covered with scrapes and cuts.

The man searched for a pulse. None. But then Tommy moaned. He was alive.

The man raced back to the road and began trying to flag down a passing car. Traffic was heavy but nobody stopped. Finally, the man covered Tommy and sprinted for a nearby house in the rain. He pounded on the door.

"Call an ambulance!" he told a frightened woman.

The man raced back to the boy's side and told him help was on the way. Within 10 minutes, police, paramedics and an ambulance were on the scene. Tommy was rushed to a hospital. Police took a statement from the man. Then, into the rainy night, he was gone.

Meanwhile, Tommy fought for his life. Among other injuries, he had a fractured skull and a torn spleen. He underwent emergency surgery for the ruptured spleen. Doctors told his stepmother they weren't sure he would survive.

He did. But in the recovery room, his lung collapsed. More surgery. Finally, Tommy was stabilized. By the time the man was back home in Washington, Tommy was awake, alert and able to remember everything.

Everything, that is, except the accident itself. Police suspected it was hit-and-run. The woman who had phoned the police said that five minutes before the man came to her door, she had heard the screeching of brakes. Someone had gotten out of a car, then quickly gotten back in and raced off.

The boy's stepmother wondered why nobody else had stopped to help her son. The bike had been in plain sight. "In this day and age, very few people will pull over and help someone," she said. "People don't want to get involved. That man's efforts saved my son's life. That's what the doctors told us. The timing factor was critical."

Because of the heavy traffic, it was estimated that 50 to 75 cars had passed by her son before the one man stopped. Some undoubtedly never even saw the bicycle and, thus, never considered that someone might be in trouble. But you have to think a number did see it, yet continued on their way.

Why did this one man stop? "I'm a Christian," he said, when contacted about the incident, "and we're called to help other people."

"Good Morning America" will not be calling on him. What he did won't be seen as heroic as rescuing a child from a well or pulling an airline flight attendant out of an icy river. On a dark, wet, country road, he simply became a 20th-century Good Samaritan. He helped when others would not, risked when others played it safe.

And taught at least one other person—me—a lesson. The ebb and flow of day-to-day life is not nearly as dramatic as the scenario involving this boy and this man. And yet each day, we see little signs that someone might be in trouble.

Do we simply drive by, assuming that all is well? Or do we take the risk to pull over and see if we can help?

CHAPTER SIX

Trading Style for Substance

The song accompanying the television commercial touted a food product designed as a return to "home cookin'." And what was this new form of "home cookin'?" A TV dinner.

The trendy sociologist alluded to what she called "non-monogamous" marriage. And what was she referring to? Adultery.

The seminar leader told audience members how they could find success in the workplace. And what was her profound advice? "Natural fibers," she said. "You are what you wear."

Welcome to the age of style over substance, pomp over pithiness, charisma over content. This is a time when who we are has become less important than who people *think* we are; when euphemistic phrases can seemingly turn wrongs into rights; and when politicians are often judged more on their charisma than on their convictions. Bluntly, what you see ain't always what you get.

In 1990, the German "singing" group Milli Vanilli had its Grammy award withdrawn after it was discovered the duo had only lip-synced its songs. If that was interesting, so was a comment from one of its members, Rob Pilatus, who probably didn't realize the double meaning when he said, "We really love our fans—we just hope that they understand we were just young and wanted to live life the American way."[1]

From the triviality of TV dinners and lip-syncing to the seriousness of abortion and infidelity, the American way often means selling beautifully packaged lies. And as it becomes increasingly difficult to separate the counterfeit from the real, we're increasingly reaching for our wallets. What's worse, we're starting to wrap ourselves in those same beautiful packages and forgetting it's the content that counts.

This insane obsession with image works against the reality that God intends for us. It muddies an other-oriented Christian value system with the me-first murkiness of Madison Avenue. We subconsciously substitute real virtues such as honesty, humility and forgiveness for cosmetic replacements such as designer clothes, bigger houses and "perfect" bodies. Our teenage children get pushed to conform at all cost. Mothers at home question their worth because they don't fit the briefcase-toting image of success. Our churches become more concerned with denominational pride than becoming a haven for the "poor in spirit."

Though the media have fueled the style-over-substance syndrome, the phenomenon is nothing new. In biblical times, the Pharisees were champions at creating the image that they were pure and holy. In fact, they were merely robe-clad forerunners of the dress-for-success movement—people whose outer appearance didn't necessarily reflect their inner selves. They loved to pray, give to the needy and fast—all in front of others. Their motive was obvious: not to selflessly serve God and others, but to *convince others* that they were selflessly serving God and others.

As image becomes more important, what the image hides becomes more irrelevant. A convicted rapist objected to a book written about him. "It made me out to be some sort of failure," he said. "How could (the author) say that? I had five $400 suits; I had a $600 watch; I drove a Toronado."[2] His image had superseded his actions and become like some all-purpose cleaner that—at least in his mind—wiped away even the toughest grime.

And why not? Hasn't TV taught us that romance blossoms from wearing the right kind of perfume? That the right hair conditioner is a prescription for popularity? That we should buy a particular brand of pills because, while the author touting them isn't a *real* doctor, "I play one on TV."

Lest you think we don't fall for such rubbish, consider this: In the first five years of the "Marcus Welby" TV show, more than 250,000 people wrote letters to Robert Young, the star of the show, most of them asking for *medical advice.*[3] We've become so anesthetized by image that it's becoming more difficult to choose the real from the fake.

Insignificant as it might seem, the home cookin' commercial is a perfect example of this intentional blurring of reality. The image is of a homespun meal: Huge helpings. Fresh-from-the-garden vegetables. The kind of dinner Grandma used to make on the family farm. But the image is more than a distortion of reality; it is a 180-degree lie. In fact, the food was thrown together on a conveyor belt by people who probably live across the country. And what do we really get? Small portions in an aluminum tray that come to us not fresh from Grandma's oven, but not-so-fresh from the supermarket freezer.

The fact is, marketing executives would not be using the home cookin' image unless they knew we were gullible enough to fall for it. And we are. Is it any surprise that many of us also buy into deceptions with much more serious consequences?

The same sales job employed by the TV dinner people is also employed by the pro-abortionists: Let people believe they're getting one thing (personal rights) so they won't stop to consider another thing (an unborn baby's death). The goal is simple: If you emphasize home-cooking long enough, people will forget they're eating frozen food. If you emphasize loss of rights long enough, people will forget unborn infants are dying. If you use all the official rhetoric—"equality," "choice," "reproductive freedom"— then, just as rock-hard biscuits can be passed off as Grandma's finest, so can abortion be passed off not only as ethically acceptable, but downright dignified.

If pro-abortion forces honestly believed that a baby in its mother's womb were only a mass of tissue, why do they cry foul when anti-abortionists use photographs of an unborn baby? Because, in a very graphic way, such photographs bare a truth that cannot rationally be denied: That is life inside that womb. Image can create a lie, but substance always reveals truth.

Rather than risk a philosophical U-turn, however, many people prefer rationalization. Or, better yet, rule-changing. Don't like the implications of something? Change the rules. Widen the playing field to convince yourself you're in bounds even if you're not.

That's what the International Olympic Committee did in 1988. At the time, the Olympic charter clearly stated that "the use of the (Olympic) emblem for advertising alcoholic beverages or tobacco is *strictly* prohibited." (Italics mine.) But a brewing company had put the five Olympic rings on its beer cans, a brewing company that, not incidentally, was spending millions of dollars to promote the games in Calgary. The committee deliberated, then announced its ruling: beer and wine, it said, weren't actually alcohol so the company could leave the Olympic logo on its beer cans.

It's the same philosophy that more and more churches are using so parishioners—and pastors—can shirk accountability; instead of exhorting people to turn from practices that the Bible says are wrong, the churches simply rationalize that such practices are right. For such churches, truth isn't the Rock of All Ages, but 20th-century Silly Putty, an elastic substance that can be stretched and stretched until it conforms to personal comfort zones.

Another way our culture changes the rules is to change the language. "Adultery" sounds so very *wrong*. That's precisely why some sociologists have substituted the "nonmonogamous" term—because, they say, it carries no connotation of good or evil. Their switch represents yet another step into moral neutrality.

Through language, we cheapen that which is good and enrich that which is not. "Making love" is now euphemistically substituted for any act of sex, regardless of whether love played a part. What used to be "chastity" is now "neurotic inhibition." What used to be "self-indulgence" is now "self-fulfillment." Such pre-sweetened phrases represent the foundation of the image-over-substance philosophy: Don't change your ways. Don't change your heart. And, above all, don't feel guilty. Instead, simply change the image of your actions.

So, how do we combat the image-idoling that's intensifying around us? Most importantly, by finding a role model to pattern our lives after. We need look no further than Jesus himself. He needed no public relations firm. He simply lived His values, doing what He knew was right, obeying His father, sacrificing for others. He was open. He was honest. He was holy. His virtues were reflected in the choices He made, the words he said, the promises he kept. Ours should too.

Said Jesus: "Woe to you, teachers of the law and Pharisees, you hypocrites! You clean the outside of the cup and dish, but inside they are full of greed and self-indulgence. Blind Pharisee! First clean the inside of the cup and dish, and then the outside also will be clean" (Matthew 23:25-26).

Jesus saw so clearly the foolishness of the world. He refused to go with the cultural flow, choosing instead to follow His father. "Watch out for false prophets," said

Jesus. "They come to you in sheep's clothing, but inwardly they are ferocious wolves. By their fruit you will recognize them. Do people pick grapes from thornbushes, or figs from thistles? Likewise, every good tree bears good fruit, but a bad tree bears bad fruit" (Matthew 7:15-17).

If seemingly righteous people can actually be unrighteous, seemingly ordinary people can actually be extraordinary. When I think of people of substance, I don't necessarily think of CEOs or people featured on magazine covers or people with lots of money or people with lofty academic degrees. Instead, I think of a Sunday school teacher sitting at her kitchen table on a Saturday night, trying to make a scale model of Noah's Ark with popsicle sticks. I think of the mother and father who get up at 5 A.M. every day to get their disabled son ready for school. I think of the woman who cleans the church alone on Saturday nights.

Jesus didn't hang out with the chosen class. He interacted with lepers and the blind, prostitutes and Samaritans. Likewise God used seemingly ordinary people who had weakness like you and me: Moses, a man with a speech problem, and Mary, a woman without notoriety. In choosing a King, God passed over the older sons of Jesse and chose the unlikely David. "The Lord said to Samuel, 'Do not consider his appearance or his height, for I have rejected him. The Lord does not look at the things man looks at. Man looks at the outward appearance, but the Lord looks at the heart'" (1 Samuel 16:7).

We need to be authentic, transparent people, willing to share with others our hopes and fears, our weaknesses and worries. When we pretend that life is bliss or are afraid to let down our guard, we encourage those around us to do the same—and thereby destine ourselves to superficial relationships. Only if we're vulnerable can we hope to establish relationships that reward. Only if we're real can we hope to get to know the realness of others. It's interesting that we feel closest to one another during crises, perhaps at the funeral for a loved one or in the midst of a serious illness. Why? Because we take off our masks of invincibility and share our true selves.

My wife and I met a couple from church. They were a handsome couple, both blond, and carried an air of success, as if straight from the pages of a Land's End catalog. From time to time, my wife and I would make small talk with them before or after services. We would ask how they were; they would say fine. My wife got to know the woman better at a weekly Bible study. They invited us to a prayer breakfast and I remember I'd never seen a couple look so chipper and well-groomed at 7 A.M., so *together*, not only as individuals but as a couple.

It was the last time we saw them. No, they didn't die. But their marriage did. The two of them stopped coming to church and we soon discovered why: They were getting divorced. The incident left me not only saddened, but full of regret. The couple had so carefully masked any hint of pain that we had timidly assumed there was no pain. I regret we didn't risk going beyond the surface "how-are-yous." And I regret that by the time we found out how this couple really was, it was too late; a family was no longer a family.

Taking off the masks is difficult, because the world—and, sadly, often the church—rewards those who appear to have it altogether and snubs those who do not. The image game conforms us to the world and cheapens us as people of God, who validated our worth by creating us.

"When you give to the needy, do not announce it with trumpets, as the hypocrites do in the synagogues and on the streets, to be honored by men," said Jesus (Matthew 6:2). Likewise, He said, "When you pray, do not be like the hypocrites, for they love to pray standing in the synagogues and on the street corners to be seen by men. I tell you the truth, they have received their reward in full. But when you pray, go into your room, close the door and pray to Your Father, who is unseen" (Matthew 6:5).

No amount of image-makeover can change the real us any more than a paint job can fix a car needing an engine overhaul. Such changes come only from the heart. And, unlike the claims of image consultants, they don't happen in a weekend seminar. They happen through the power of the Holy Spirit and in a lifetime of commitment to God.

To buy the world's images instead of God's substance is to go through life eating TV dinner after TV dinner—only to discover too late that we never tasted genuine home cookin'.

Pop Youngberg, Farmer

ॐ

On a windy hill above a patchwork quilt of barns, orchards and freshly plowed fields, they buried Pop Youngberg last week.

No, he's not anyone you'd know. In fact, beyond his family—he's my wife's grandfather—and the folks of Yamhill County, Oregon, few ever heard of the man. His obituary isn't particularly impressive. He never was president of this or on the board of that.

But he needs to be remembered. For the Pop Youngbergs of the world are a vanishing breed—and our fast-and-frantic world can learn from their legacies, obscure though they may be.

In a time when the average American moves 30 times in his lifetime, Pop died in the same house in which he was born 89 years ago. The average American male will hold 10 jobs in his lifetime. Pop held one: farmer. The average American couple remains married nine years. Pop and Gram were married 60.

To Pop, life was a simple trilogy of tilling the earth below him, worshiping the God above him and loving the family around him.

His life would seem to be monotonous—14-hour days on a turtle-slow tractor. But he embraced farming as something good and natural and honorable. Years after he was too old to even walk to the chicken coop, he still awoke at dawn, ready to begin the daily chores.

He never had a business card, never got a promotion and rarely took a vacation. But like his Swedish parents who tilled the same soil, he loved the family farm with a quiet passion and knew that's where he must die—in the white house shaded by the giant maple tree at the end of the long, gravel lane.

Three weeks before his death, his words came slowly and with great strain. But he had something to tell me: The faucets on the farm needed wrapping with duct tape and newspapers so they wouldn't freeze when winter arrived.

He didn't learn that by reading a book or attending a weekend seminar. After nearly nine decades on the farm, he knew when to do things almost instinctively, like a squirrel knows when to gather nuts. And he knew that when the morning fog started hanging low on the ridges of the Coast Range, winter was coming, which meant wrapping the faucets with duct tape and newspapers.

Pop made decisions based on the changing of the seasons, the word of fellow farmers and the dogeared Bibles that lay in virtually every room in the house.

He was a smart man, but not smart in the way the world thinks of. He never earned a degree, never went to college, never took a SAT. But he was a master of self-sufficiency. When he needed drawers for bolts and screws, he didn't head for the store, he took tin snips and cut turpentine cans in half. For Christmas gifts, he'd make wind chimes for his grandchildren and pocket-size board games for his great-grandchildren.

He knew what was important in life. What mattered, he figured, wasn't making more money, owning more possessions and becoming more important. What mattered were his fields, his family and his faith.

There was a naturalness to him—a realness— that's no longer stylish in our dress-for-success world. When he sang *Amazing Grace* on Sunday mornings at the tiny Baptist church in nearby Carlton, he was inevitably off a few keys. (O.K., more than a few keys.) When he dressed up, his tie was inevitably crooked. But that was just Pop. And when you looked down the pew and heard him singing, you knew that all was well with the world.

He wasn't dynamic or dashing; his standard outfit was overalls, a faded jean jacket and a hat stitched with a logo from a fertilizer company. He often had a toothpick dangling from his mouth.

His hands were large and calloused; his heart large and tender. At the dinner table, he'd ask family members to hold hands during the prayer and after he'd said "Amen," he'd give your hand a squeeze.

His eyes always said more than his words. When family members said goodbye after a visit to the farm, his eyes would grow misty.

Well-intentioned relatives gave him calculators, Instamatic cameras and the like for years. He was too polite to refuse them, but most such gifts wound up on a shelf somewhere, seldom, if ever, used.

A month before Pop died, a cousin and I were talking about computers. Pop sat there in his chair, the wall clock ticking incessantly in the background. And I wondered: What must he think of this talk about disk drives, megabytes and parallel ports?

This is a man who was 49 years old when the first electric typewriter was introduced. A man who lived through the reign of 19 presidents. A man born into a world of horse and buggies and whose body would be taken to the cemetery in a baby blue hearse.

In the weeks before his death, he gave away many things to relatives: a button hook he had used to fasten his shoes, a driver's license with a June 30, 1937, expiration date—things that made you realize how ill-fit he was for the world of freeways and fast food.

But the greatest gift he gave was simply being Harry "Pop" Youngberg, farmer. For the seeds he scattered in his lifetime grew much more than just wheat, strawberries and corn. And, in the family he left behind, those seeds promise to bear fruit, despite the winds of change.

Letters of Love

🐦

*I*t *was 1944* and she was away from home for the first time, having left the farm on the prairie of south-central Minnesota for nursing school in Minneapolis.

Each day, the dormitory's house mother would arrange the newly arrived mail alphabetically on the lobby coffee table. Marge would immediately look in the left-hand row—her last name began with B— and, at least once a week, see it: a letter from her mother.

Now, 45 years later and three time zones away, she walks outside her condominium, opens the mailbox and, at least once a week, sees it: a letter from her mother.

In a world where style has become paramount, it's often the substance in the shadows that's most inspiring. A 63-year-old woman. Her 85-year-old mother. And a commitment to a relationship. Two people linked by love and letters.

"Our closeness," says Marge, "has come from the words we've exchanged."

They started writing when postage stamps cost three cents. In five different decades, spanning three wars and the death of both women's husbands, the letters have continued—thousands of them. "You don't measure mom's letters by the page," says Marge. "You measure them by the pound."

Esther, Marge's mother, sometimes writes about the early days when she and her husband were trying to survive the '30s on a farm with two infant children. "Before the Depression you lived life," she says. "Afterward, you *fought* it."

Kerosene lamps. Water fetched from a well. Hot summers. Cold winters. Drought. No car. And precious little money. "I didn't even own a purse," says Esther.

But Marge remembers a different childhood. Not bliss, but a warm family, a high school class of 13 and a mother who shared the piano bench on Mills Brothers tunes. "I didn't know we were so poor," she says.

At 18, Marge left for nursing school. "When she left for Minneapolis, it was like cutting off one of my arms," says Esther. "My husband would come in and I'd be crying and he'd wonder why. I'd tell him my little girl has left and I'm lonesome."

So, too, was that little girl. Thus began the letter writing. "The mailman would come down the road about 9 o'clock every morning," says Esther. "I'd be thrilled to death if there was a letter from my daughter."

"Her letters kept me afloat," says Marge.

Soon, there were letters to Mom about a special boy Marge had met, later about plans for marriage, still later about her pregnancy. She ultimately had three children. Esther came and stayed when her grandchildren were born and returned when they were sick and Marge needed help. "She's always been there when I needed her," says Marge "And I've had a lot of needs."

In 1962, after mother and daughter moved to Oregon, Esther's husband died of cancer. It wasn't the last time the disease would call on the family. In 1969, Marge had a mastectomy. Three years later, her husband died of cancer. Mother and daughter found themselves alone, together. "It was a very tough time," says Marge.

After Marge moved five hours away, the two continued their letters. Marge now writes on weekends and mails Monday. Esther receives on Wednesday and writes that night.

The letters include all sorts of topics, from the trivial to Marge's latest bout with cancer. "Life started with her and I can't imagine not including her in everything I do," says Marge.

She writes about 10 pages on a steno pad; her mom responds with at least a couple dozen. Sketches of happy faces and musical notes accompany the words.

"She has a need to tell people things and I'm glad I can be there to meet the need," says Marge. "Maybe in 20 years I'll need my children to do the same for me."

Someone once observed that a 20-year-old mother is 20 times as old as her child when the baby is 1. At 40, she's only twice as old. And at 80, she's only $1\frac{1}{3}$ times as old. "She's 63 and I'm 85 but in many ways we're the same age," says Esther.

They are now more like long-distance friends

than mother and daughter. Grown-up pals who, whether together or apart, have struggled through a Depression, disease, death and the day-to-day challenges of life.

Why? Because they have been willing to be open and honest. Because they've built a mother-daughter friendship based on the nitty-gritty of real life instead of trading "all-is-fine" superficialities. And because on a clear September day nearly half a century ago, before climbing on a Greyhound bus and leaving home, a daughter promised to write. And when she did, her mother always wrote back, each letter beginning the same way.

My dearest . . .

CHAPTER SEVEN

Trading Promises for Perseverance

One Saturday morning, my son went out to play with two of his friends across the street, just as he does most Saturday mornings. On this day, though, his friends weren't around. They had left with their father for the weekend so their mother could pack her belongings and move out of the house. Their parents were getting divorced.

"Why is she leaving?" my son asked, at age five not understanding the ways of the adult world. According to the sociologists, psychologists and futurists, I was supposed to tell him that the American family was simply changing with the times, taking on new forms. Breakups were inevitable. Once-and-for-all marriages simply aren't practical anymore. And with a little therapy, his friends would survive the transition as if it were little more than a rearranging of the family's living-room furniture.

"I guess your friends' parents couldn't get along," I said, then watched as the mother drove away for the last time.

That such scenes occur is tragic enough. What's equally tragic is that, in the supposedly back-to-the-family '90s, marital split-ups merit little more than a shrug of society's shoulders. It's as if we've lowered our standards rather than elevated our concern. In a country supposedly bent on the pursuit of excellence, in marriage we often settle for "fair" or "poor." If half our state governments, major businesses or schools failed, we'd be in a panic. But when half of all first marriages end in divorce, too many of us accept it as some sort of scheduled stop on the flight to fulfillment.

Rather than reevaluating our commitment, the cultural norm is to rationalize the lack of commitment. Reported *U.S. News and World* report: "Tomorrow's children will grow up with several sets of parents and an assortment of half- and step-siblings. Futurists believe that the prevalence of divorce will make it less of a burden on parents and children. The psychological trauma, moreover, may be greatly reduced."[1]

The futurists obviously didn't ask the opinions of the 18-year-old street kid I once interviewed, a boy whose mother had been married and divorced four times. "Divorce tears kids apart," he told me.

The futurists also must have overlooked the 22 ninth-graders—most from divorce situations—whose short stories I was asked to critique. Free to write about anything they wanted, 15 dealt with the subjects of divorce, death, murder, suicide or abandonment. Sounds to me a whole lot closer to psychological trauma than the happy days the futurists foresee.

The U.S. divorce rate is the highest in the world. The average U.S. lawnmower lasts longer than the average U.S. marriage, which makes it to 9.4 years before folding.[2] For the first time in history, Americans who marry today are more likely to lose a spouse through divorce than through death.

Today, nearly half of marriages are *remarriages* for one or both partners, suggesting that, despite past failures, people are drawn back to this union. But if second marriages suggest a certain hopefulness, reality rains on the parade. The chances of a second marriage surviving are considerably worse than for a first; two-thirds of second marriages end in divorce and chances for survival decrease with every subsequent remarriage.[3]

What such statistics show is that changing partners is not the answer. It's easy to blame marriage as restrictive or a spouse as uncaring. It's easy to blame the stresses of children, finances and jobs. What's difficult is to look ourselves in the mirror and accept that we might just be part of the problem. And to accept that, though well worth the adventure, marriage wasn't meant to be some sort of magic carpet ride through turbulent-free skies.

"Previous generations were taught that life is hard, sacrifice is necessary, and unhappiness a cross that sometimes must be borne," wrote Landon Y. Jones, author of *Great Expectations: America & The Baby Boom Generation*. "But the baby boomers were not willing to make the risky and often painful compromises their parents did. Just as they had great expectations for themselves, they had great expectations for their marriages. Life was too short to live with an unhappy marriage. If they could switch to another TV channel, why not switch husbands or wives?"[4]

Never mind that the next channel probably won't satisfy, or the next or the next. In the '90s, expect a resurgence of rationalization that now-and-forever marriages just aren't the answer. Already, novelist Rona Jaffe, whose works have sold more than 23 million copies, has written a book suggesting that such relationships are yielding to what she calls "sequential monogamy," a euphemistic term for what amounts to marriage a la carte. Instead of long-term commitments, she says, society will shift to a series of short-term relationships.

What people such as Jaffe fail to realize—or, more accurately, are unwilling to admit—is that such setups will only compound frustrations, not create fulfillment. The answer to unfulfilling relationships isn't changing channels and isn't changing our partner to be more like us, but being changed into the person God wants *us* to be. Those who move from relationship to relationship fail to realize who's the common denominator in the equation.

Alas, Christians are increasingly turning to divorce as an answer. One day I got a call from a woman who had seen a newspaper column I'd written on marriage. A Christian, she attended one of our city's more respected evangelical churches, where her husband had been an elder. They had been married 19 years when he suddenly announced that he was leaving her and their three kids for a younger woman. Since then, I've learned of a number of couples— some of them friends—whose relationships have been similarly shattered.

It's difficult to so forcefully oppose divorce when you have friends who have gone through it. "We are caught in a dilemma," wrote sociologist William Donohue. "No one but the most cruel would want to inflict psychological distress on men and women who are in the process of divorce; they deserve our understanding, not imprecations. It therefore seems compassionate to do everything we can to remove the last vestiges of stigma from divorce. But the rub is this: By weakening the social penalties attached to divorce, we necessarily occasion more of it."[5]

Divorce was once seen as a panacea. When no-fault divorce arrived 20 years ago, it was hailed as a quick solution for soured marriages and a victory for women. But study after study shows that it backfired. The feminization of poverty is the major result of no-fault divorce; after a marriage ends, the man's income increases by about 30 percent and the woman's decreases by essentially the same amount. Only about half of divorced fathers pay the full amount of their child-support.

What's more, children of divorce often get physically disconnected from one parent and emotionally disconnected from both. Over half of kids from single-parent families see their father less than once a month, including

31 percent who never see their father at all.[6] The mother is often still embroiled in bitterness with an ex-husband, which emotionally drains her and her children. She usually must work outside the home, meaning she has little time and energy for her kids. And the father often loses touch with the children. "Almost half of children of divorces enter adulthood as worried, underachieving, self-deprecating and sometimes angry young men and women," wrote psychologist Judith Wallerstein in her landmark book, *Second Chances.*[7]

The street kid I referred to earlier had an amazingly perceptive view of what he'd been through. "Adults," he told me, "don't understand how emotionally vulnerable children are."

His mother and father were divorced when he was young, and his mother proceeded to go through three more marriages. "I wanted to know why I didn't have a father. I'd ask my mom. She never would answer in a way I could understand, because every answer I wanted had a happy ending. I've been harboring anger ever since."

In a desperate attempt to get someone to pay attention to him, he turned to drugs. "Things like that are a cry for help," he said. "Divorce tears kids apart. Is it easy for a kid to love somebody and then have that person leave? You find yourself asking, 'Don't you still care? Don't you still love me?'"

Nobody, in taking a vow of marriage, expects the relationship to fail. So why do half of all marriages fizzle? Largely because of a fuzzy understanding of what God intends the relationship to be. In Ephesians 5:21, Paul speaks of the need to "submit to one another out of reverence for Christ." But, culturally, we seem to view marriage in two distinct—and misguided—extremes. Some look at marriage in knight-in-shining-armor terms, a fantasy land of romance, bliss and idealism that never considers the reality of moods, habits, changing needs and changing diapers.

Others look at marriage as a well-negotiated business deal in which two people try to secure promises that *their* needs will be met. Devoid of any sense of sacredness, such marriages become day-to-day renegotiations of a contract that will never be satisfactory, a contract that speaks of compulsion, not commitment; legalism, not love.

What about unconditional love? We want 50-50 relationships when they require 100-100 commitments. Today, we talk of irreconcilable differences, a term that suggests the virtual impossibility of repairing a relationship on the rocks. But is it really an impossibility? Or is it simply pride? Is it really irreconcilable differences or is it two people hurling blame rather than facing shortcomings and, with God's help, trying to overcome those shortcomings?

What about perseverance? If any generation would seem to have an excuse for giving up on marriage, it would seem to be the one that weathered the Depression, a time in which economic hardship didn't mean going without designer labels but sometimes going without dinner. Yet the divorce rate actually went down in the '30s.

Relationships are like running a race: They reward not those with the best style, but those who endure, those who see the pain as part of a process. Unfortunately, too many of us quit when we first feel a cramp. A 1973 cartoon from *The New Yorker Magazine* has proven to be prophetic; it showed a minister saying to a bride and groom: "To relate, respect, and yet be your own person, until, perchance, affections erode?"

Once, I interviewed a cyclist whose $2,500 bike attested to how seriously he took the sport. A 43-year-old computer software technician, he mentioned he was recently divorced. I asked why. He told me bluntly that bicycling broke up the marriage. He loved the sport. His ex-wife did not. Thus, he said, they split. In a country where marriages have survived wars, poverty, sickness and disease, welcome to hardship, baby-boom style.

What about promises? They are the foundation of many relationships. We promise our children we'll take them fishing. We promise friends that we'll write. We promise our bosses we'll get the job done. But in no other relationship is the promise more important than in marriage, which is the foundation of society.

True, it's difficult keeping promises in a society that places so little importance on follow through. But with God's help, it can be done. Beyond the marriages I've seen broken, I've seen an equal number mended. And the reason was recommitment to Him, which naturally leads to recommitment to others.

We need to see marriage not as a relationship we create one day with a wedding, but as a relationship we create each day with work. Not as a way of molding our partner to be like us, but of helping him or her become all God wants him or her to be. Differences are what make us unique creations of God; if we're searching for a partner who will be just like us, we will never find the treasure.

Our marriages will improve if we emphasize fewer promises and more perseverance, less drama and more delivering. What if, as an experiment, we put as much effort into relationships as we did into our jobs, hobbies, church volunteering or daily workouts? Such a commitment begins with a promise, but is nurtured by daily discipline. "Let us not love with words or tongue but with actions and in truth," we're told in 1 John 3:18.

It's easy to love someone when times are good. But times aren't always good. When I want inspiration for my own marriage, I think of two friends whose God-centered marriage withstood the loss of their two-year-old son to leukemia, the type of stress that usually splits up couples. In such times, knights in shining armor mean nothing; neither does a tidy marital contract. In such times, the key to survival is not warm, fuzzy feelings but cut-to-the-bone commitment, both to God and each other.

In serving each other, husbands and wives serve God. We're to accept each other not based on some unattainable list of conditions, but unconditionally—through good times and bad, in sickness and in health, yes, even if one of us enjoys bicycling and one does not.

It's time we reflect on those wedding promises, not only to see if we're still making good on our pledge, but to remember the words of 1 Corinthians 13, a chapter whose wisdom captivates in the midst of a candlelight ceremony but too often fades in our day-to-day lives.

"Love is patient, love is kind. It does not envy, it does not boast, it is not proud. It is not rude, it is not self-seeking, it is not easily angered, it keeps no records of wrongs. Love does not delight in evil but rejoices with the truth. It always protects, always trusts, always hopes, always perseveres."

Behavior, not words, changes people. Love isn't saying "I do." Love is proving it with an unbroken promise.

Divorce
War

&

"*All rise.*"
The gavel falls, the judge sits down, the trial begins. Six years ago in a church, the couple had said "I do" to each other. Now, in the stark coldness of a courtroom, they begin the painful process of saying "I don't."

Sitting within 15 feet of each other, the man and woman avoid eye contact at all costs. Though legally still married, they have become petitioner and respondent, not husband and wife; enemies, not allies. The connection between them is as lifeless as the bricks on the courtroom walls.

"Just think," says a court reporter between sessions, "they once called each other sweetheart."

We've all watched a marriage begin, but few of us have watched a marriage end. From the back row of the courtroom, I've come to watch such an ending, to witness one of the divorce wars fought in hundreds of courtrooms across America each day. It isn't pretty. But, then, to understand the importance of wearing a seat belt, sometimes you need to look at a mangled car.

The man and woman, whom I chose at random, are your typical middle-class family. They're nice-looking and dress well. They're not part of a dysfunctional family, a counselor has ruled. They're simply a couple who decided to split up because of "irreconcilable differences."

A judge will decide who will get everything from their house to their Funk & Wagnalls encyclopedias. But the big question is who will get custody of their three-year-old son.

As the trial unfolds, a chasm of contrasts separates then and now, wedding and dissolution. The two are flanked not by a best man and maid of honor bearing rings that will unite but by attorneys armed with evidence that will divide.

There is no photographer capturing each priceless memory, only a court reporter recording each verbal volley.

There is no triumphant music, only the tinny sound of testimony spoken into microphones.

There is no festive throng of family and friends, only empty benches and a handful of supporters waiting in the lobby.

Between sessions, the two gather with their friends and families in the lobby, like boxers going to their respective corners.

The woman's attorney argues that the man is an irresponsible parent, as shown by the raising of his 12- and 14-year-old sons—his by a previous marriage—who lived with the couple. He doesn't believe in structure and discipline. He doesn't care if the kids do their homework or not. The woman, the attorney says, has cared enough to set boundaries, build structure and require accountability.

The man's attorney counterattacks. He argues that the woman has been abusive to the children.

She has hit them, screamed at them, locked them out of the house in their underwear. The man, he says, has cared enough to help the boys with their homework, calmly handle friction and cook an abundance of meals, particularly pancake breakfasts.

On topics ranging from pearl necklaces to dented trucks, from flunked classes to stapled cats, the attorneys continue their assaults, dropping smart bombs to do damage in strategic positions. Pierced ears, paddles and broken pickle jars—these are among the subjects that come into play in deciding which parent would be best for a little boy who has no say in the matter.

At one point, the woman is on the witness stand. "You talk about a time when (your husband) put you into a bedroom," says her husband's attorney.

"He threw me into the bedroom, yes."

"Do you remember why you were placed in the bedroom by him?"

"He was angry at me."

"Do you know why?"

"No."

"Wasn't it because he just separated you from having a fight with one of the older children?"

"No."

Minute by minute, hour by hour, day by day, the evidence grows like a gnarly tree. The judge hears about the time the three-year-old was slapped for pushing the VCR buttons during *The Little Mermaid*. The time he cried when being shifted from one parent to another. And the time he was allowed to ride in the back of a pickup truck.

What's true? What's not? Amid this family's chaos, it's difficult to tell. While the battle continues, the propaganda war heats up, each side describing incidents in vastly different ways.

For a few days, the two older boys' neighborhood friends—ranging from age 9 to 14—come to testify. They gather excitedly in the lobby, as if on a Cub Scout field trip. But their moods grow serious when, one by one, they are brought into the courtroom; nervous kids in dress shirts and ties and Nikes, innocent kids caught in the cross fire of warring adults.

Timid, their words on the witness stand are barely discernible. While cross-examining the boys, the woman's attorney impatiently taps his fingertips together. He places land mines to trip up witnesses who step in the wrong spot and, for those still unscathed, fires a machine-gun of questions to crack their credibility.

Between sessions, one of the young witnesses looks at the stockpiled ammunition on the attorneys' tables, piles of notes and documents.

"This," says the little boy, "is a mess."

When the seven-day trial finally ends, the court reporter has typed the equivalent of 1,400 double-spaced pages. The judge has listened to about 30 witnesses. The attorneys have entered 110 pieces of evidence, everything from belts allegedly used for hitting to father-son photographs. And the man and woman have spent about $35,000 in attorney's fees; one attorney charges $95 an hour, the other $145.

Two weeks after the trial ends, the judge, "with considerable trepidation," grants custody of the child to the mother and gives the father liberal visitation rights. In his decision, he mentions a recent case in which the state had to remove a child from the care of a mildly retarded man and woman. The couple had tried courageously to overcome their handicaps and be good parents, but it was not within their capacity. How sad, the judge points out, that two mentally sound people can hardly do better.

"For a variety of reasons, I hope never to see another case like this one," he says.

As the courtroom empties and the parties return to their new lives, you wonder how the same people who promised themselves to each other six years ago could become such bitter enemies. You wonder if it was all worth it; if divorce is, indeed, the great mender of wounds that it was hailed back in the '70s. And, finally, you wonder about the collateral damage of ending a marriage in the trenches of a trial.

What has this taught the older children about how adults solve family problems? And what will become of the three-year-old who, as the judge says in his decree, has been "ping-ponged" between two feuding parents?

The sad irony is this: The time and place to prove one's proficiency as a parent isn't during a divorce proceeding in front of a judge but in a family setting in front of the children themselves. For all the time, money and energy that went into this trial, all it has really proven is the high cost of divorce—in terms of money and human casualties.

In the end, the most profound statement of the trial came from the little boy who surveyed the scene and pronounced it a mess. His comment was echoed by an adult witness of the carnage.

"This is worse than war," he said. "In war, at least you have a winner."

Against
All Odds

❧

*F*ifty years ago, on a warm day in Butler, Mo., James and Lou handed a justice of the peace two bucks and vowed to love each other for better or for worse.

They got the worse.

Today, we married types complain about the hardship of juggling careers, kids and Mastercard payments. It was never that simple for Jim and Lou, not when you start your marriage with $5, you're both teenagers and neither one of you got past 11th grade. Not when your first home is a dirt-floor tent, when you spend your honeymoon working at a sawmill and when you go job-hunting on freight trains. Not when an accident puts your husband in a coma for a week, your son is born retarded and, when you finally build your dream house, it has to be moved.

"We've come a long way from that $5," said Jim, a hint of Midwest farm drawl in his voice.

No, this couple didn't become wealthy, start a chain of successful franchises or coauthor a bestselling book. They did help open the first school for the mentally retarded in the state of Washington. And they did become foster parents to a handful of children.

But perhaps their greatest accomplishment has been staying married for half a century despite odds that would have sunk most marriages. They made a promise and kept it.

When the couple started out, they didn't have access to marriage seminars, psychotherapists or paperback how-tos. All they had was love, the Lord and a will to stay together, regardless of what came their way.

And plenty came.

They met in 1936 at a church conference in Iowa, where Jim was raised. He was 19; Lou was 17. With the conference over, 300 miles separated the two. But Jim couldn't forget about the Missouri farm girl, so he hitchhiked to see her. After that visit, he scrounged up $50, bought a 1926 Chevrolet coupe and went to propose to her.

Five people showed up for the wedding, including Jim and Lou. Lou's father, not excited about losing a daughter he cherished, refused to come. But he did give the couple $5, which was all they had to start their married life.

At the time, the country was still in the throes of the Depression. An uncle gave Jim a job in his sawmill. Jim worked six days a week, made $14 a month and was nearly killed when a steam engine exploded.

Later, in Kansas City, Jim was riding down the street on his motorcycle. A car hit him from behind. He flew 25 feet in the air and skidded on the pavement for another 25 feet. "My head went through the grill of a car's radiator," he remembers.

His landlord phoned Jim's mother in Iowa to report that he was dead. He wasn't, of course. After a week in a coma, he regained consciousness and was greeted with the news that somehow—he still doesn't understand how—he had been arrested for reckless driving.

In 1940, Jim and Lou were living in the basement of her folks' house in Nevada, Mo., where Jim would walk five miles to his dollar-a-day service station job. One Saturday night, he came home from work, slumped in the chair and told Lou, "There's got to be something better in the world."

The next morning, they packed their bags and began a four-month trip to Seattle, hitchhiking and hopping freight trains. Once, they were riding in the back of a watermelon truck that crashed. They survived. Another time, they were nearly beaten by club-wielding "railroad bulls," brawny men hired by the railroads to keep uninvited passengers off the freight trains. They survived.

From North Dakota to Spokane, Wash., they rode the rails; train whistles became a familiar sound. They worked their way to Seattle by picking apples.

In Seattle, Jim got a job in a lumber mill. But he was laid off when World War II started. He found a job as a pipe fitter in a shipyard and, after four years, was able to afford the couple's lifelong dream—a home. Jim built it himself, painstakingly nailing every board in place. But before the house was finished, the state announced that a new freeway was going to be built right through their living room.

The house was moved. A few months later, as the two were finally enjoying the fruits of their labor, disaster struck: The house burned down. The local newspaper interviewed Jim at the time. "Well, we started our married life in a tent," he told the reporter. "I guess we can do it again."

And, of course, they did. Soon, they were blessed with a son. He was born mentally retarded. But Jim and Lou didn't wring their hands and become recluses. Instead, they founded a school for teaching children with disabilities, the first in the state.

Their son is now married and living with his family in another city. Jim and Lou are retired.

"The Lord," said Jim, "has been good to us."

The two keep busy by putting on free square-dance parties in a small dance hall they added onto their house. Lou bakes cookies. Jim, complete with cowboy boots, does the calling.

On Sunday mornings, they drive disabled children to church in a van that Jim customized himself to accommodate wheelchairs.

They attribute their half-century of marriage to some simple things. "Learn to give and take," said Lou.

"Think of the other person," said Jim.

They celebrated their 50-year anniversary by renewing their vows at their church. And by remembering what they went through to get there.

"Every now and then we'll hear the whistle of a freight train," said Jim. "We just look at each other and smile."

CHAPTER EIGHT

Trading Compromise for Commitment

You would never know it by watching the smiling kids on the minivan commercials or the coziness of the "Cosby Show" or by looking at all the polls and surveys in the women's magazines. But America's commitment to children is disintegrating.

"We are the least family-oriented society in the civilized world," wrote Dr. T. Berry Brazelton, a pediatrician at Harvard Medical School. "If you asked any citizen, 'Does America believe in families and children?' the answer would be 'Of course.' But how much denial and distortion is couched in that answer?"[1]

"We give the family lots of lip service in this country," an early-childhood education teacher told me recently, "but we don't prove it in our actions."

Today's generation of parents is the first in American history to allow others to raise its kids. After speaking at a grade school recently, I was intrigued to see the day-care vans parked out front, ready to take some children from school to the next step in their day away from home. The biggest influences in many children's lives today are not mother and father, but day-care workers, television and videos. We have become a generation that raises children like it dry-cleans its clothes: We pay someone else to do it for us.

It is not that children aren't important to us; it's just that they aren't a priority. It's not that we've abandoned them; it's just that we've wedged them into overcrowded daily planners as if they were little more than a hair appointment. Nobody decides, "I'm going to neglect my children." It happens slowly, insidiously, cumulatively, like the clutter in a 10-year-old's room. One day it's clean; a week later, you need a high-powered leaf blower to find the bed.

The nation's pro-family lobbyists are threatened by an intensifying anti-family faction. But an equally serious enemy may be the apathetic majority. Recently, a middle-aged college football fan was being interviewed on TV. He was boasting to the reporter that he was so devoted to a particular team that he had passed up his son's wedding to attend a game. The reporter asked him why he would do such a thing. "I love football," he said.

I'm forever seeing surveys that show overwhelming support for the family. But if families are such a priority, why does the average working couple spend only 30 seconds a day talking to their children?[2] Why has the Index of Social Health for Children and Youth, based on a 100-point scale, dropped from 68 to 37 since 1970? Why, when 30 years ago the psychiatric field of childhood depression did not even exist, are as many as 7.5 million children now suffering from some form of psychological illness?[3]

Had you walked into Room 120 of a high school in 1965, the teacher would have been teaching geography or math; 25 years later, it's Interpersonal Development, a euphemistic title for a class designed to help drug-addicted kids. As I observed the class on a mid-December day, I thought of a more innocent time, when a child's holiday challenge was resisting the temptation to open a present, not trying to stay sober. Suicides among those ages 15 to 19 have almost tripled since 1960.[4]

So much for the blissful youth theory. Children are getting lost in the shuffle of careers, marital conflict and a lack of commitment from parents. Nine out of 10 baby boomers say family is the most important thing in their lives. But, reports *American Demographics* magazine, "few baby boomers have made any career sacrifices for their family."[5]

Researcher Daniel Yankelovich has identified a large baby-boom group he calls The New Breed. When asked if they agreed with the statement "Parents should *not* sacrifice in order to give their children the best," 43 percent of the New Breed agreed, compared to only 16 percent of Traditionalists, comprised mainly of older adults.[6]

Who are the children who wind up suffering? They are rich children, poor children, black children, white children. They're the kid down the street whose father has time for everything—elder board meetings included—but no time for his daughter. And they're the teenager I know whose Porsche-driving father couldn't even tell me what high school his son attended. In some cases, they're your kid. And, in some cases, they're mine.

As adult children of alcoholics are painfully learning, the scars of youth do not always disappear. Unlike a Dec. 31 tax write-off, the time we didn't spend with our child years ago cannot be made up in a day. The demand for perfection that we heaped on our child for years cannot be undone overnight. And the divorce that was supposed to end all problems is often just the beginning.

Isn't it time we stopped compromising and, instead, recommitted ourselves to our children?

To do so, we must appreciate what's important in the everyday lives of those children. Take a child's school play or a teenager's soccer game; as an adult, it's easy to dismiss it as insignificant, a drop in the bucket of time. But life is made up of such drops. Those drops are like the drops of rain that create a high-mountain creek, a creek that becomes a stream, a stream that becomes a river, a river that becomes the oceans that cover three-quarters of the earth. What may seem insignificant today becomes very significant when multiplied by time.

By not making children a priority we allow them to become less and less a part of our lives. I tend to throw myself into projects at work, sometimes without counting the cost. But the other day, I was reminded of the cost: My desk had become a pile of books and papers and reports. And back in a corner was the picture of my two sons, buried beneath it all. Like a cold splash of water, the scene awoke me to where my children had been shoved on my priority list.

Sometimes, we parents rationalize our lack of involvement with our children. They don't really need us, we might say. But that's not the case. "Sociologists have begun to realize . . . that teens are more dependent on grownups than was once believed," said a *Newsweek* essay. "Studies indicate that they are shaped more by their parents than by their peers, that they adopt their parents' values and opinions to a greater extent than anyone realized."[7]

To accept that doesn't mean to subscribe to parent-bashing. But it does mean facing the realization that a 1-800-KIDTALK number or a "Home Alone" coloring book just doesn't cut it when a child has a problem and her workaholic parents aren't around to help. If our children seem to be growing up with an absence of positive values, it could well be that we're not taking the time to transfer those values. Children do not bounce back from divorces, separations and marital discord like the indestructible warriors who continually rematerialize in kids' video games.

The idea isn't to agonize over what we've done wrong—we serve a forgiving God—but to ask ourselves what we can do to make things right.

I recently took my two sons camping for a weekend, orchestrating the trip with the precision of an orchestra conductor. The tent had to be exactly where I wanted it. Meals had to be at precise times. Fishing was to be taken seriously. Midway through the weekend, I found myself seething because not all was going according to my master plan. Our neighbors were too loud. The fishing stunk. I'd forgotten the can opener.

Then I realized something: Playing in the lake for hours without a break, the kids were oblivious to all that was going wrong; they were too busy having fun. It was their father who had the problem, because he hadn't taken his sons camping, he had taken himself camping and brought his boys along as bit players in his own production. Once I faced that reality, once I confronted myself, I was able to relax, refocus and do what I should have done in the beginning: Let this be the children's weekend, not mine. Loosen up. And laugh at my utter failure as a fisherman. In doing so, I found a new sense of contentment.

Consistent with the baby-boom generation's penchant for either living in the fast lane or dropping out altogether, many have pushed parenting to dangerous extremes. Either we become the great orchestrator, plugging our kids into this program and that class for our own benefit, or we become the distant parent, a voice on the phone, the eyes behind a newspaper, the note on the refrigerator.

In 1990, the number of children being raised by grandparents would fill nearly nine Rose Bowl stadiums; in the '80s alone, the number jumped an incredible 50 percent.[8]

The extreme example of the former are the thousands of parents for whom kids have seemingly become little adults. Wrote one baby-boom parent:

> We are, I am told by educators, the most difficult group of parents they've ever had to work with. We worry about everything; we analyze

and stew and get second opinions and read books and come to each situation prepared with lists of questions. . . . What has happened is that we have brought the tools that helped us gain success in careers to the task of parenting. We are competitive, time-efficient; we run on schedules and so do our kids; we believe in doing things right and want our kids to have the right tools; and we're concerned that with children you can never start anything too early.

We compress their time and pack it with play dates, lessons of all kinds and enriching experiences such as camping and skiing. I can't help asking what worlds will they have left to conquer.[9]

The irony is that we parents tend to heap on our kids everything *we want* but little that *they need*. The further irony is that in both cases—the dropout parent and the overzealous parent—the missing ingredient is attention. "Focused attention, in my experience, is the most demanding need a child has," wrote Dr. Ross Campbell.[10]

Such is reality. If we're genuinely concerned about children, we need to be equally concerned about what environment offers the best opportunity for their growth and development.

An ABC "Prime Time Live" program in June 1991 aired a shocking litany of neglect in American child-care centers. Its undercover cameras captured scenes such as one worker trying to watch 17 kids, a year-old child being so neglected that he finally fell asleep on a kitchen floor, babies spending entire days in their car seats. Certainly, quality child-care centers exist. But as *Reader's Digest* says: "The deepest problem with paid child-rearing is that someone is being asked to do for money what very few of us are able to do for any reason other than love."[11]

Sixty percent of mothers with children between the ages of three and five work outside the home, according to the Bureau of Labor. Working outside the home is a necessity for many mothers, particularly single mothers. But, for many, it is clearly a choice. Though some rationalize they cannot survive on a single income or pass up every promotion offered, that's often because our "standards of survival" have skyrocketed. In 1988, the Roper Organization queried 600 Americans whose household income was more than $100,000 about what they considered necessities to living: Seventy-nine percent said they "couldn't live" without a microwave oven, 49 percent couldn't live without a telephone answering machine and 36 percent couldn't make it without a VCR. The kicker? Only 30 percent said they "couldn't live" without quality education for their children. [12]

It comes down to priorities. Granted, few of us make more than $100,000. But I would imagine we all have similar items we would list as necessities. The point is painfully clear: Many of us seem unwilling to give up luxury items for ourselves in exchange for necessary time with our children. The question isn't, "Can we afford to live on less?" but "Are we willing to live on less?"

For women, the decision to work outside the home is not an easy one. There's nothing wrong with finding fulfillment in a job. But if there are benefits to careers and second incomes, there are costs as well. Disconnecting a career to raise a family doesn't necessarily mean you can't reconnect the career later, when children are grown. However, parents who put children on hold too often return later— much later—to find the line has gone dead. Children who lose touch with parents will make their connections elsewhere.

Brazelton, the Harvard pediatrician, worries about the disappearance of discipline, particularly when both parents work. He also is concerned that working mothers are so overwhelmed by guilt that they "detach from the baby, because it's the only way of coping."[13]

It is not anti-woman to suggest women spend more time with their children, anymore than it is anti-man to suggest men do the same. Men who constantly work overtime and spend weeks on the road seem to believe they have been granted a parental waiver, as if families must orbit around a job. Perhaps it's time men consider their priorities, too. Promotions certainly offer benefits, but at what cost? What kind of salary can compensate for eroded relationships? Why is the pursuit of excellence reserved for the workplace? How ragged must family life get before we make radical changes in our priorities?

Children are desperately seeking stability, to feel they belong. If they don't find it in the home, the director of a home for unwanted children recently told me, they will certainly find it elsewhere: on the streets, in gangs, in cults, perhaps even in jail, all of which serve as surrogate families.

As the issue of families finds its way into more magazines and onto more television time slots, I find myself applauding this long-overdue recognition of the problem but decrying the pass-the-buck nature of the solutions. Schools must pick up more slack, we're told. Businesses must put in day-care centers. Government must fund more children's programs.

All three might, indeed, help brighten the situation. But what children really need is not three more hours in a schoolroom, wondering when Mom or Dad might come for them. It's not just a day-care down the hall from mom's office. It's not just an improved child-care tax credit. What children need today are living, breathing, live-together parents for whom children are more than just another scrawled name on the To Do list.

Instead of talking about what schools, business and government can do, it's time we considered what we can do. For in today's family drama, there are no good guys and bad guys. Just too many scripts with sad endings.

Coming Home

ॐ

*I*t's January, a new year, that annual time when we recommit ourselves to such lofty goals as giving up Double-Stuffed Oreos, changing our car's oil at regular intervals and cleaning the sludge out of the gutters.

In other words, a time for recommitting ourselves to trivial things. Which is why I'm writing about a woman who recently recommitted herself to something much more important than diets, cars or gutters—her family.

In our stress-for-success society, it's not uncommon to see families sacrificed on the altar of upward mobility. But it's rare to see the opposite.

Which brings us to Sharon, a 41-year-old woman who did exactly that. Two years ago, it seemed, she had it all: a house in the suburbs and a management job with a worldwide computer firm.

"I was caught up in the American Dream," she said.

But, beneath the facade, she was caught up in a nightmare. She and her husband were on the brink of divorce. Her daughter, an eighth-grader, was involved in drugs.

So Sharon did an uncommon thing: She quit a $40,000-a-year job to help save her family. She kissed a career goodbye—at least temporarily—to reacquaint herself with a 14-year-old bundle of fascination and fear. She gave up the white-collar world of ladder climbing for the blue-collar chore of rebuilding a crumbled relationship with her husband.

"I can always go back to work and take my Honda back on a trade," she said, "but I'm not going to give up my kid and husband."

What intrigues me about her story is that this is not a woman who dreaded work and was looking for an out. This is a woman who thrived on it. She managed 17 software writers. She was good—and knew it.

But she carefully weighed the alternatives: She could keep pounding the corporate treadmill, losing sight of her family in the process. Or she could get off the treadmill to fix her fragmented family, and perhaps lose the chance to get back on.

She chose the latter. "I was told by most of my peers that I'd committed professional suicide," she said. "There's not a man in the business who would take me seriously now."

After leaving her job, only two colleagues have remained friends. The others, she says, have snubbed her as a quitter, as damaged goods, as weak.

But that's alright, she says, because she's discovered, for the first time, life outside the office. When her daughter was in kindergarten, the teacher had asked the students to answer the question, "What does your mommy do?" Her daughter had written, "My mommy makes money."

Now, Sharon realizes her daughter was not growing up with a mother, a role model—but with a stranger who carried a briefcase and occasionally came home to pop something in the microwave.

"We were a family in a hurry," she said. "For the first time, we now have an event that occurs every night between 6 and 8—we call it dinner. There's a sense of normalcy in the house. We do old-fashioned things like talk."

The transition was not easy for anybody, particularly Sharon's daughter. She had liked having the house to herself. She had liked what mom's salary meant to her wardrobe.

But her drug problem signaled that freedom and big bucks were hardly the keys to contentment.

Sharon knew that quitting her job wouldn't instill the home with Leave-It-to-Beaver bliss. "But my daughter needed to feel cared for," she said. "The drugs and alcohol were a symptom of a larger problem."

For the first time, Sharon learned who her daughter's friends were—and which ones were bad news. She opened the house to the responsible friends. And set down some hard-and-fast rules for her daughter, penalizing her when they were broken.

Most of all, Sharon listened. And observed. "Sometimes, you don't need to say anything, you just need to be there," she said.

If she had taken the time to do that before, she says, she would have noticed the glazed look in her daughter's eyes when she was high on marijuana. She would have noticed when her daughter had boyfriend problems and needed someone to talk to.

In doing so, Sharon has become more than just someone who makes money. She is a mother—and proud of it. Her marriage is improving. And she has established a freelance editing business in her home.

And what if she hadn't quit work? "My daughter would have run away, and my marriage probably would have fallen apart."

That, she decided, was a price she wouldn't pay.

Big Life

ﻬ

"**G**o, *baby, go, baby, go!*"
"C'mon, faster, faster, get goin'!"

The sound of my two sons, then six and three, was coming from the patio as I worked in my office at home a few years ago. What I needed was quiet. What I got instead was children cheering. But cheering what?

"What's going on out there?" I asked, mildly miffed at the noisy intrusion.

"Nothin', Dad," said my six-year-old. "We're just racin' caterpillars. Wanna race one?"

I politely declined, explaining that I had *important* stuff to do. But in the years since then, I've learned a simple, but profound, truth: Racin' caterpillars is important stuff, too. Real important stuff. As parents, we need to be willing to get down on our hands and knees and experience life from our children's perspective.

That's not easy, I know. We are—ahem—adults. We are involved in what my youngest son calls Big Life. We pay taxes, tie Windsors, speak four-syllable words, fight traffic. Then, suddenly, some freckle-faced six-year-old in a dinosaur sweatshirt is asking us to *puh-leeze* play freeze tag with him.

So we do what any self-respecting parent would do: We squirm out of it somehow:

🍂 "Too tired." (Of course, we weren't too tired to put in another three hours of computer work on the Petersen deal later that night or watch a couple of sitcoms.)

🍂 "How 'bout if I just stick in a video for you?" (No wonder a recent study showed the average five-year-old spends 25 minutes a week in close interaction with his father and 25 hours a week in close interaction with the TV set.)

🍂 "How about tomorrow, sport?" (By the time tomorrow comes, the kid won't be asking us to play freeze tag, he'll be asking for tuition money to Stanford.)

It's almost a cliché to urge parents to spend more time with their children. But what I'm learning as a parent is that we need to spend more than just time. We need to spend "kid time." Particularly with pre-teen children, we need to step out of Big Life and experience Small Life.

Instead of reading a book on a park bench while little Mary swings, we need to be swinging next to her. Instead of watching a game of hide-and-seek from the front porch, we need to be hiding and seeking. Instead of jogging the track while the boys play soccer, we need to be out there, playing with them.

In short, we need to spend time *with* them, not just *around* them. To participate, not observe. To create our own fun, together, rather than buying it at some arcade. And, yes, to get a little wild and crazy, even if it means being the only parent in the neighborhood who sleds when it snows.

The idea isn't to forego our responsibilities as parents—teaching and disciplining our children, praying for them and modeling a good husband-wife relationship for them. The idea is to supplement such things by stepping into our children's world— not stay permanently, but just visit from time to time. Ecclesiastes 3:1 says there is an appointed time for everything. I like to think there's a time for serious talks, worship and study. And a time for piggyback rides, marshmallow fights and sleeping out back on a summer night, listening to crickets and the tat-tat-tat of the neighbor's sprinkler.

Likewise, our love for our children manifests itself not only in teaching them Christian values, but in dressing up as the Big Bad Wolf in their basement production of The Three Little Pigs. And investing time—kid time—in their lives. Writes Paul in 2 Corinthians 9:6: "He who sows sparingly shall also reap sparingly; and he who sows boun- tifully shall also reap bountifully."

Remember how good you felt as a child when Mom and Dad showed up for your third-grade open house at school? It was because they were stepping into your world, a day-to-day world where they seldom ventured. Somehow, that made you feel im- portant. For one evening every term, your parents would look closely at your stick-figure drawings and feeble attempts at cursive. They'd sit at your desk in one of those miniature chairs—knees at ear level— and see life through your eyes. That's what we as parents must do—but more than just one evening a term.

It's important to understand how adults and children see life so very differently. One summer, my boys set up a Kool-Aid stand. Seeing they had made only 60 cents by noon, I realized two things: First, I'd made a major marketing mistake by choosing to live on a cul-de-sac with no drive-by traffic. Second, while I considered their venture a failure, they considered it a complete success. To me, 60 cents meant disappointment; to them, it meant pure gold, or at least a pack of baseball cards.

Adults are results-oriented; children are process-oriented. To me, the Kool-Aid stand was only a wagon, a scrawled sign and two pitchers of Kool-Aid so thick it could pass as Jell-O. To my sons, however, it was an entrepreneurial adventure. Exciting stuff.

Adults go fishing to catch fish; children go fishing for the experience, to see how a worm squiggles, to wonder how an old tire came to rest at the bottom of the lake, to ask questions like, "Do fish go to church?"

Adults want the perfect experience; children just want fun—and tend to find it even when we don't. On a drizzly day at the coast, my wife and I sat in a restaurant, lamenting the lack of blue skies we'd eagerly anticipated for our vacation. Across the table, the boys didn't have time to be down; they were too busy having fun by breaking soda crackers into the shapes of U.S. states.

Going from Big Life to Small Life sometimes creates difficulties. Balancing the roles of Authority

Figure and Human Horse can lead to problems if your children don't understand what mode you're in at a given moment. Besides that, it can be hazardous to your taste buds, sometimes even boring. I still haven't quite forgotten the taste of the lunch I let the boys make me one Saturday afternoon; those of you who have eaten a peanut butter and ketchup sandwich know what I mean. So do those of you who have played two hours of Candyland, trying desperately to allow anyone to reach Home Sweet Home so the game would mercifully end.

But it's worthwhile making ventures into the Candyland of our children's lives. Each trip, though it may seem insignificant at the time, helps build a bond between parent and child that will last long after the game has been put away or the sled has been stored in the attic or the Kool-Aid stand has become just a wagon again.

Which is why I'm hoping the boys will give me an opportunity this summer to join them in an activity I once shunned. When they get older, I doubt they'll remember the presents I bought them or the videos I rented them. But, if they give me a second chance, they might just remember that afternoon one summer when their father's caterpillar won the Triple Crown.

CHAPTER NINE

Trading Rights for Responsibilities

Coming home from work one day, I saw a huge motor-cycle parked in my driveway. Once in the house, I discovered it belonged to the man who was talking with my wife, a bushy-bearded guy with whom I had gone to high school and hadn't seen in 15 years. We had never been close friends, but he had seen something I'd written in the newspaper, realized we lived close to each other, and come to see me.

He stayed for dinner. As we talked that evening, he told me what had happened to him since graduation. It wasn't pretty, he admitted. He had fathered an illegitimate child. He had begun and ended numerous relationships. He had been married, had two more children and gone through a bitter divorce and custody battle. He lost. He had bounced from job to job. He had become suicidal. Recently, things had been looking up because he had found a new girlfriend. She left him.

Over the next few years, we met a handful of times to talk. We talked about how the key to personal change is turning to the one who created us, not relying on ourselves. Though halfheartedly agreeing, he would back-burner that idea and begin telling me about the "if-only" solution: If only the courts would wake up and see what a wonderful father he was, he could get custody of his children and everything would be all right. If only the guy he had given $1,000 to in order to bet on a horse hadn't swindled him, he wouldn't be having financial problems. If only he could take a trip and get away from all this mess, he could live happily ever after.

So he hit the road. Every few months, I'd get a post-card from him, signed "The Drifter." They'd come from all sorts of places, wherever he could afford to get when he got tired of the place he had been. He was running but couldn't hide. He was searching for something but didn't know what. Outwardly, he was free of responsibilities; inwardly, he was enslaved by regrets.

In one sense, his experience may seem wildly different from most of ours. And yet the difference may be deceptively small. Who among us hasn't played the "if-only" game? Blamed others for our problems? "Hit the road" to run away from those problems, even if that meant emotionally distancing ourselves from a spouse, buying an expensive outfit or throwing ourselves into some recreational pursuit? In the final analysis, what my friend and the rest of us sometimes fail to do is simply be accountable for our actions. Realize that choices are inextricably tied to consequences. And understand that when we hide behind our rights, we're often ignoring our responsibilities.

Individual freedom has become a cultural idol, courtesy of the baby-boom generation. "Over the past 20 years, the idea of individual freedom has evolved like a mutated animal, involving the absence not only of significant choice but of moral or rational restraints," wrote *Time* magazine's Roger Rosenblatt. "Without a context of limitations, freedom has become dangerous and meaningless."[1]

Individual responsibility, meanwhile, has become the moral equivalent of the Edsel. Our culture offers fewer and fewer consequences for irresponsible behavior so it becomes more and more accepted.

On the trivial side, I once did a story on a woman who ran a rent-a-liar business, the last refuge of the irresponsible. For a price, she would call someone's boss, pretend she was a nurse and confirm—"fibbing," as she termed it—that her client was ill and would have to miss work. Lest you think Americans would never stoop so low, I interviewed the woman a month after she had opened for business and she had already lied for 300 people, being careful to take their money before she lied for them. (After all, who can you trust these days?)

On the more serious side, in a time when the country's population has increased only 40 percent since 1960, the number of lawyers has increased 300 percent, much of the demand created by people who, not wishing to take responsibility for their own actions, try to lay the blame on others. After falling off a fire escape, a student at a university sued a fraternity, alleging it was negligent for unlawfully providing beer to him and not supervising him better.

In 1990, rock-singer Madonna defended her latest kinky video by pointing a finger away from sex to violence. Never mind what warped ideas children could get from her video. "Why is it okay," she asked, "for 10-year-olds to see someone's body being ripped to shreds?" What was so ironic is that earlier in the year, John Russo, the maker of violent horror movies, had defended his trade by blaming such movies on "society," that catchall depository of personal blame. "If the movies reflect, with disturbing accuracy, the psychic terrain of the world we live in, then it's up to us to change that world and make it a safer place," he wrote. And Russo's contribution to that end? Among other films, *Night of the Living Dead*, the so-called grand-daddy of splatter flicks.[2]

Those of us who don't share such misguided values cannot afford to ignore them. For the more a culture's rules change, the more potential there is for us to change with them. In essence, American individualism has shifted to what sociologists call raw self-interest rather than the collectivism of other cultures. Cultures built on collectivism have among the lowest rates of homicide, suicide, juvenile delinquency, divorce, child abuse and alcoholism, according to a study done by the late Raoul Narrol, a professor of anthropology at the State University of New York in Buffalo.

"The individualism that's on the rise recently in the U.S. is one of 'What's in it for me?' with immediate gratification of one's own needs coming before all other loyalties," said Robert Bellah, a sociologist at the University of California at Berkeley. "Commitments like marriage only hold while they pay off."[3]

In the last few years, a significant number of baby boomers have turned to what New York psychologist Ronald Taffel calls "parent bashing." But while it's wrong to dismiss explorations of painful childhoods as counterproductive; and while we need to understand our pasts in order to understand ourselves in the present, how long can we use our upbringing as a crutch to avoid our own responsibilities? Life is not fair. Like ourselves, parents are not perfect. We need to forgive them and get on with it. "Blaming parents for what they did or didn't do has become a national obsession—and big business," reported *American Health Magazine*. "The children of the Me Generation had the time and money to indulge themselves in the pursuit of perfection. When their dreams began to shatter, say the experts, the boomers began to point a finger at their parents. After all, it must be *someone's* fault."[4]

I slouch. I could easily blame that on my parents, saying that although they encouraged me to sit up straight, they did not encourage me enough. But the fact is I slouch because, from the time I was young, day after day, I chose to ignore warnings from my parents and others. Now, I'm paying the price for that: my back gets tired easily and I have difficulty sitting up straight.

Beyond blaming others, we often slough off responsibilities by running away. We don't necessarily hit the road, but we do run away from the truth, hide behind our insecurities, bury ourselves in a career, throw ourselves into other people's problems, get lost in the sheer busyness of life—anything so we won't have to come to grips with who we are and how we might need to change.

Finally, we rationalize. A letter-writer in a local newspaper publicly announced that, as a divorced woman, she would no longer feel "guilt, shame or remorse" for destroying her nuclear-family Christmas. Well, that's fine; who was asking for a public flogging? But her letter went on to explain how positive it was for her children to fly around the country during the holidays, to be part of a number of family gatherings. While I suppose children could benefit from gaining "quiet wisdom about baggage claims and an experienced traveler's knowledge of schedules and ticketing techniques," they could benefit much more by being allowed to have childhoods, not adult lives fraught with anxiety and wrapped in 10-year-old bodies. Many children of divorced parents are suffering from inter-generational jet lag, having grown tired of being bounced around from home to home as a result of their parents' divorce.

Does that mean, as parents, we need to live in day-to-day regret because of what has happened in the past? No. We serve a forgiving God who's more concerned with what we can be than what we have been. At the same time, we need to live in day-to-day realization that the choices we make have consequences. Children are less interested in first-class airline tickets than in first-class parents, less concerned about how to pick up their airline baggage than what to do with their emotional baggage. True, children need an increasing amount of independence, the older they get. But as victims of parents' busy lives and marital battles, children are being forced to emotionally fly alone much too early and at a personal cost that's much too high.

In 1988, *Time* magazine reporter Melissa Ludtke lived with a handful of families across the U.S. for a cover story on America's children. She found that the baby boomers' great experiment of allowing their children to raise themselves was failing miserably. ". . . For all the work of sociologists, psychiatrists and researchers, children are best able to articulate what makes them the way they are," wrote Ludtke.[5] After four months of interviews and observations, her conclusion was this: "(Children) are looking for someone—parents, teachers, ministers—to set limits and impose discipline. Without walls to bounce against, children seem lost."

Though it sounds so appealing, the quest for unlimited freedom ignores an essential element: Freedom at its best requires restraint. In one of the great ironies of our times, the same country that extols individual liberty at all costs has been forced to incarcerate a higher percentage of its population than any other country in the world.[6]

In terms of family relationships, Rosenblatt, the former *Time* magazine editor, describes a scene in which "Mom and Dad sit planted in front of pieces of paper or *The Cosby Show*, while the children lie still as dolls on their beds and gaze at ceiling fixtures, like stations in a dream. See how free everybody is. The only thing missing are the essentials: authority, responsibility, attention and love."[7]

It's time we saw clearly that with freedom comes responsibility. We needn't rely on "self" and "feelings" to be our moral guides; God has provided that guide in the form of His Word, which defines the boundaries of right and wrong. When Christ forgave the harlot, he also admonished her to change her ways. And, in a spirit of repentance, so must we be willing to change ours.

"You, my brothers, were called to be free. But do not use your freedom to indulge the sinful nature; rather, serve one another in love. The entire law is summed up in a single command: 'Love your neighbor as yourself' " (Galatians 5:13-14).

To serve means to sacrifice, to die to self, to put someone else's needs above our own. It is impossible to love if we're always blaming, impossible to serve if we're always running, impossible to sacrifice if we're always rationalizing. Are we willing to give up the hallmarks of a generation—freedom and self—and accept the hallmarks of God—commitment and responsibility?

To do so might mean forgiving a parent for hurt they caused you as a child. Or taking the first step in repairing a relationship with a friend. It might mean pulling back on a hobby you love until your children have left home. Or, for both men and women, rededicating yourself to serve your spouse.

Too often, we see love as a way of getting what we want. In fact, love is giving what others need. It is not just some warm, fuzzy feeling that shatters when someone slams the door. It is not a capricious tug that ebbs and flows like the tide, depending on whims and moods. Instead, it is the embodiment of all those words that sound so very threatening, so very serious, so very grown-up to a generation that wanted to stay forever young: responsibility, commitment, accountability, sacrifice, forgiveness.

They are the words none of us heard on our stereos in the '60s and '70s. Instead, we heard that love will bring us together, that love could take us higher, that all you need is love. But never understanding love at its deepest and most demanding level, too many of us have become like my friend The Drifter, running from responsibility, moving on when we get tired of the last place we've been, all the time wondering *if only* . . .

Belonging

❧

*W*ith the freeway ahead of us and home behind, the photographer and I left on a three-day newspaper assignment. We were bound for the Columbia Gorge, where the Columbia River carves a mile-wide path between Washington and Oregon; where windsurfers come from across the country to dance across waves created by "nuclear winds"; where I would be far from the world of nine-to-five and deadlines and routines and errands and rushing kids to baseball practices and having to make sure my socks weren't left on the bedroom floor.

Far away from the R word—responsibility.

Frankly, it had not been the perfect farewell. Our family was running on empty. Our '81 car was showing signs of automotive Alzheimer's. We were all tired, cranky, trying to shake colds.

My eight-year-old son tried to perk us up with his off-key version of a song from the musical, *Annie*: ... *The sun will come up tomorrow; bet your bottom dollar that tomorrow there'll be sun.*

It didn't work. I had been busy trying to get ready for the trip; my wife Sally had been busy fretting because my three days of freedom were going to cost her three days of extra responsibility.

"Daddy, are you coming to hear my class sing Thursday night?" Jason, my eight-year-old, asked amid the chaos of my departure.

Had I been Bill Cosby, I would have gotten a funny expression on my face, said "Well, of course," and everyone would have lived happily ever after—or at least for half an hour.

But I didn't feel much like Bill Cosby that morning. "I'm going to be out of town," I said. "Sorry."

Giving Sally a quick kiss, I was on my way. Now, hours later, I was far away from family, free from the clutter, the runny noses, the demands on my time.

Knowing little about each other, the photographer and I shared a bit about ourselves as we drove. Roughly my age—mid-30s—he was married but had no children. He and his wife had seen too many situations where couples with children had found themselves strapped down, scurrying for baby-sitters and forced to give up spontaneous trips.

He told me how he and his wife had recently taken a trip to The Gorge by themselves. My mind did a double take. *By themselves?* What was that like? Long ago, in a universe far, far away, I vaguely remembered what that was like. Taking off when the mood hit. No pleas for horseback rides about the time you're ready to crash for the night. No tornado-swept rooms. No meet-the-teachers nights.

Besides having no children, the photographer had no six-month old French fries on the floor of his car, no legs of Superman action figures on his dashboard and no road maps on which most of Idaho had been obliterated by a melted Snicker's bar.

Where had I gone wrong?

For the next couple of days, despite a threat of rain, we explored The Gorge—thousand-foot walls of basalt rising on either side of the Columbia; fluorescent-clad sailboarders, like neon gnats, carving wakes in the water.

If the land and water were intriguing, so were the windsurfers. There were thousands of them, nearly all of them baby boomers, spending their days on the water, their nights on the town, their mornings in bed.

Every fourth car had a board on top. License plates from all over the country dotted the streets. Some of these "boardheads" were follow-the-wind free spirits who lived out of the back of vans; others were well-established yuppies who were here for a weekend or vacation.

In the evenings, the river's hub town turned into Oregon's version of a California beach town: boomers eating, drinking and being merry, lost in a world of frivolity and freedom.

For me, seeing this group was like discovering a lost, ancient tribe. You mean, while I was busy trying to put on jammed bike chains, these people were jamming to the rock beat of dance clubs? While I was depositing paychecks to be spent on groceries and orthodontics bills and college funds, these people were deciding what color sailboards to buy?

Where had I gone wrong?

On our last night, the cloudy weather continued, which irked the photographer and mirrored the mood that had overcome me; we both needed sunshine, only for different reasons.

As I stared from the motel room at the river below, I felt a sort of emptiness, as if I didn't belong. Not here. Not home. Not anywhere. Just as the winds of The Gorge were whipping the river into whitecaps, so were the winds of freedom buffeting my beliefs. Faith. Marriage. Children. Work. I had anchored my life on such things, and yet now found myself slipping from that fixed position. Had I made a mistake? Had I sold out to the rigors of responsibility? Someday, when I was older, would I suddenly face the brittle-cold reality of regret, wishing I had gone with the wind?

I was getting ready for bed when I spotted it—a card in my suitcase, buried beneath some clothes. It was from Sally. The card featured cows—my wife's big on bovines—and simply said, "I'll love you till the cows come home."

I stared at the card for minutes. I repeated the words. I looked at the same handwriting that I'd seen on love letters in college, on a marriage certificate, on two birth certificates, on a will. As I went to bed, there was no need to call the front desk and ask for a wake-up call; I'd already gotten one. The card bored through my hardened heart, convicted my selfish conscience, refocused my blurry perspective. I knew exactly where I needed to be.

The next day, after a two-hour interview, six-hour drive and three-block sprint, I arrived at my son's school, anxious and out of breath. The singing program had started 20 minutes before; had I missed Jason's song?

I rushed into the cafeteria. It was jammed. Almost frantically, I weaved my way through a crowd of parents clogging the entrance, to where I could finally get a glimpse of the kids on stage.

That's when I heard them: 25 first-grade voices try-ing desperately to hit notes that were five years away.

. . . The sun will come out, tomorrow; bet your bot-tom dollar that tomorrow there'll be sun . . .

My eyes searched this collage of kids, looking for Jason. Finally, I spotted him: Front row, as usual, squished between a couple of girls whose germs, judging by the look on his face, were crawling over him like picnic ants. He was singing, alright, but with less enthusiasm than when he's been told to clean his room.

Suddenly, his eyes shifted my way and his face lit up with the kind of smile a father only gets to see in a grade-school singing program when his eyes meet his child's. He had seen me, a moment that will forever stay frozen in my memory.

Later, through a sea of faces, I caught sight of Sally and my other son. After the program, amid a mass of parent-child humanity, the four of us rendezvoused, nearly oblivious to the commotion surrounding us. I felt no emptiness, only connect-edness.

How could one man be so blessed?

In the days to come, I resumed my part in life as bike-fixer and breadwinner, husband and father, roles that would cause a windsurfer to yawn. But for all the excitement of riding the wind, I decided, I'll take the front-row smile of my eight-year-old son. And for all the freedom of life in The Gorge, I'll take the responsibility of caring for the woman who vowed to love me till the cows come home.

A Lesson Learned

૨૦

A *year ago* at this time, my wife and I were worrying about which fourth-grade teacher my oldest son was going to get. Ryan, then 9, could explain a zone defense and tell you most of the Seattle Mariners' batting averages, but wasn't headed for anybody's All-American academic team. And looming in front of him was a teacher reputed to be a drill sergeant in a dress.

Her name was Miss Sofie. Upper 40s. Never married. And known to give homework as if Ryan's elementary school were Harvard Law and she were Professor Charles W. Kingsfield of "Paper Chase" fame.

"Let's put it this way," said one father whose son had had Miss Sofie the previous year. "She gave a geography quiz on the last day of school."

Gulp.

My wife and I contacted the school's principal and asked that Ryan not be placed in Miss Sofie's class. He wasn't. We were relieved.

But a few days into school, the class Ryan was in was deemed too large; some students would have to be shifted to Miss Sofie's class. Ryan was among them. We were petrified.

On the day I walked Ryan into Miss Sofie's class, I felt as if I were Abraham taking Isaac up the mountain to the sacrificial altar.

Ryan didn't say much for a few weeks. Then one evening, as we finished dinner, he abruptly took his plate to the kitchen. "Time to hit the books," he said. I nearly spit out my milk. As the school year unfolded an amazing thing happened: Ryan fell in love with learning.

In the months to come, he learned the location and spelling of countries and cities I'd never heard of. He learned to organize his time, do homework, do research. He learned to count to 10 in Norwegian. Recite poetry. Spell. Write. Weave. And figure the Mariners' batting averages without using a pocket calculator.

Above all, Ryan learned to be responsible. Because he was being taught by a woman who understood the importance of responsibility.

As the school year wound to a close, Miss Sofie didn't show up one day. Later, she missed a week. The news ultimately hit like shattered glass. Cancer. But knowing her feistiness—this was a woman who played the accordion and once lived in an Israeli kibbutz—we figured she would be back in the saddle come September, inspiring a new class of kids to memorize Carl Sandburg's *Fog* and to find Mozambique on a map.

But she never came back. She died in July.

"You don't replace a Sherrie Sofie," a minister said at her service. "God threw away the mold."

Ryan was heartened to know that, as a Christian, Miss Sofie was safely in heaven, but crushed that she was gone. "I don't think I'll ever have a better teacher," he told me after hearing the news.

Not everybody was as fond of Miss Sofie. Some found her too rigid, too demanding, too domineering. But they were the exceptions, not the rule. "Miss Sofie's class was the last place I learned any geography," said one ex-student. "I had a lot of good elementary teachers, but she stands out."

At the memorial service, many echoed such sentiments.

"She was pretty much a traditionalist," said a fellow teacher.

At school, after recess, girls in Miss Sofie's class entered the room first. If the flag salute wasn't done well, it was done over again.

After the flag salute, the class would sing a patriotic song—*The Star Spangled Banner* perhaps, or *America the Beautiful*. Each day, the class ran at least two laps around the field.

She believed in music, memorization and manners. She abhorred students saying *yep, nope* and *um*. If a child used too many *ums*, Miss Sofie would politely remind him, "We don't speak ummish here. We speak English."

When the class went to the library, Miss Sofie ranked its behavior on a 1-to-10 scale. "Six and 7 were satisfactory," Ryan said. "But Miss Sofie wanted 8, 9 or 10."

For Miss Sofie, wrong was wrong and right was right. She was like the basketball coach in the movie *Hoosiers* who demanded the ball be passed so many times before a shot was taken; he knew it might look senseless to others but it would breed what the team needed most: teamwork and discipline.

"Her philosophy was: 'You only get what you expect,'" said a fellow teacher. "She did not adhere to 'I-can't-do-it' philosophy and showed children they *could* do it."

Said Ryan, "She believed in me."

Miss Sofie seemed like someone out of the '50s, but you couldn't argue with the results. Good penmanship was a must. Deadlines were to be met. Johannesburg was not only to be located, but spelled correctly.

Once, a boy with behavioral problems advanced threateningly toward Miss Sofie, a chair raised over his head. She disarmed him in an instant. "She was one of the few people I knew who didn't compromise," said a fellow teacher. "I thank her for that. We compromise too often these days."

She loved kids. She loved to see them succeed, overcome, persevere. And she loved to laugh. She was the life of the teacher's lounge. "Sherrie never entered a room quietly but always with a flourish," said a teacher. "She'd whisk over to the piano, start to play and insist that we all sing."

On Washington's Birthday, she would bring homemade cherry pies for the staff. She started a Grandparents Day at the school. And her class parties were better organized than most time-management seminars.

This summer was supposed to have been a recovery summer. It wasn't to be.

Miss Sofie would often remind her class that learning wasn't easy—and I suppose that's true whether the subject is math or geography or life or death.

But because of her, a nine-year-old boy whose favorite book was the *Seattle Mariners Facts Book 1988* is now reading *The Secret Garden*. And the boy's father has learned something about judging people without even knowing them.

Ryan will hold fast to his memories, and I to mine. In particular, I'll remember Miss Sofie on the day my wife and I showed up early for a parent-teacher conference. We found her alone in the classroom, playing *Bicycle Built for Two* on the piano with Carnegie Hall passion.

Now, she is gone. But for anyone who's ever had a Miss Sofie as a teacher, the song goes on.

CHAPTER TEN

Trading Fantasy for Faith

For all the devious ploys used by those who create television commercials, one thing about them can't be disputed: Advertisers know what appeals to people. In a word, fantasy. "Live the fantasy," whispers the voice on the perfume commercial. The right beer turns an arid desert into a cool party, complete with swimming pool and bikini-clad women. The right car turns the mousy, bespectacled young woman into a freewheeling swinger. The right soft drink turns the feeble great-grandmother into an action-packed octogenarian.

As the 20th century winds to a close, such commercials represent only a small portion of the way we fly away on the wings of fantasy. On the more serious side, drugs, alcohol and mysticism are among the ways people escape the "real world." Television offers us a wide range of fantasy, from MTV's obsession with sex and violence to Robin Leach's glorification of the rich and famous.

To be sure, some of this represents an innocent foray into the imagination. But much of it is something else: a calculated compensation for something missing from our lives. In fantasy, we try to find what reality hasn't provided. In fantasy, we attempt to find the missing pieces from our life's puzzles. But for many, it never quite fits. They've reached mid-life with a high level of achievement matched by an equally high level of anxiety, and find themselves struggling to discover something that supersedes money, prestige, power, even freedom: meaning.

In a sense, many baby boomers are like a cast of characters looking for a plot. "They are looking to connect again, to feel linked to something," said Ann Clurman, vice president of Grey Advertising. "We're a little bit turned off from glitz and puffery. We're looking for some of the things we can count on...."[1]

Some have turned to spiritualism, but not spiritualism anchored in the historical Jesus. Instead, New Age religion—though actually quite old—has offered baby boomers a sort of spiritual smorgasbord that includes everything from past-life regression to visualization to soul travel to astrology.

What's interesting is that this is the skeptical generation. "We grew up old," said author Joyce Maynard. "We are the cynics who see the trap door in the magic show, the pillow stuffing in Salvation Army Santa Clauses, the camera tricks in TV commercials."[2] And yet these same cynics not only eased into the New Age as if it were a comfortable pair of slippers, but willingly shelled out big money to buy crystals and tarot cards and astrology charts and learn about karma and chakra and inner selves and higher selves.

For all its glitzy accessories, the New Age movement boils down to expensive self-worship, encouraging participants to focus not on others and certainly not on God, but on themselves. Many have embraced the New Age not by design, but by default. "When people no longer believe that their country is powerful and benevolent, that the family can be a source of enduring unity and support or that a relationship with God is important, where else can they turn for identity, satisfaction and hope?" wrote Martin E.P. Seligman, a University of Pennsylvania psychology professor. "Many people turn to a very small and frail unit indeed: the self."[3]

Do you see the paradox? If it were true that finding life's answers inside naturally translates into peace and contentment on the outside, why, then, is this generation so full of angst and discontent? If *we* are the answer, if *we* are powerful enough to be our own gods, why, then, have so many of us succumbed to the power of addictions? Why can't we make marriages last? Why does this generation have the highest suicide rate ever? Why do our children feel such a need to escape with drugs?

For previous generations, happiness was a by-product of doing something well; it wasn't pursued as an end unto itself. But for boomers, it has become exactly that, a compulsive search on a trail of books and tapes and techniques and treatments and seminars and causes and movements and gurus and money-back guarantees, all of which begin repeating themselves after a while. And so we become like the cartoon character who appears to be running fast; upon closer inspection we realize it's the background that's actually moving and, despite the illusion, the character is simply running in place, going nowhere.

For this generation, there's always been something better out there. In college, we switched majors to try to find it. Later, we switched mates, friends, jobs, therapists, locations, philosophies, hobbies, causes, hair styles, body shapes—anything to find The Secret.

In 1990, *American Demographics* pointed out that three out of four Americans had fulfilled most all of their material needs. "So what's next?" the magazine asked. "Americans may have all the widgets they want, but what they haven't had enough of is fun."[4] And what, you wonder, will we seek after we've had enough fun? And what will replace whatever replaces fun? And on and on and on.

Like impatient TV watchers, remote controls in hand, we click from one program to another, trying to find one that satisfies. In the meantime, such endless searching extracts a heavy price. When we thought escape was the way to fulfillment, we became drug addicts; when we thought money and materialism were the ways to fulfillment, we became workaholics. Food. Sex. Shopping. In so desperately seeking one thing, we became slaves to another thing. The number of support groups in America has quadrupled in the last 10 years; 15 million Americans now meet weekly in such groups, most of them to break free from some sort of addiction.[5]

Amid such struggling, God, for many, has become little more than an extension of the imagination, something to mold into whatever we want. Some have molded Him into nature itself; no longer is He seen as the maker of the seas and the stars and the mountains. Instead, God *is* the seas and the stars and the mountains. For some, the earth, though deserving of our utmost respect, has become an idol. It's nothing new. "They exchanged the truth of God for a lie, and worshipped and served created things rather than the Creator," we're told in Romans 1:25.

Some have molded God into a spiritual servant, ready to come should we ring for Him, but not allowed near us otherwise. In an article about baby boomers and religion, *Newsweek* referred to pastors in the '90s who have "airbrushed sin out of their language.... Heaven, by this creed, is never having to say no to yourself, and God is never having to say you're sorry."[6]

For others, God has become nothing more than a think-positive placebo, a figurehead for human hope, a source of unlimited power cast blithely aside while we cross our fingers. If we think positively, say some, we can create our own reality. If we hope hard enough, perhaps it will happen. If we rely on our feelings, who needs faith? If *we* do this; if *we* do that. In putting our trust in self, we become like people who take cover under a lone tree during a lightning storm, unaware that in their quest to find safety they have actually chosen the most vulnerable place to be.

For the unbeliever, the challenge lies in understanding that God is the very essence of meaning, the real thing in a world bent on fantasy. What people are really struggling for is a sense that they matter—and to the God who created them and loves them unconditionally, they do. Earlier in the chapter, a marketing expert referred to baby boomers' growing need to connect, to feel linked to something. That link is Christ, who came to connect with a wayward world. No glitz. No puffery. Instead, someone to count on, for both the beggar and the head of the board.

It's understandable why a generation jaded by assassinations, Watergate and wars might be hesitant to reach beyond itself. It's hard to trust when you feel you've been betrayed. But in a turbulent world marked by selfishness and seduction—sadly, some of it coming from those calling themselves Christians—God is the one unbroken promise. No fine print. No payment due. Instead, someone to believe in, even for those who have been let down by others.

It's also understandable that boomers brought up in an authoritarian home believing God was some sort of celestial cop would be hesitant to establish a relationship with Him. But the image of God as the ultimate bad guy doesn't jibe with the substance of Scripture, which speaks of a loving God. No tyrant. No heavenly hall monitor. Instead, someone who's forgiving, even for those who don't think they're forgivable.

In Christ lies the strength to make others, not self, our priority. In Christ lies the peace and freedom that many so desperately seek. He offers not temporary peace, as the world offers, but lasting peace that can end an addiction—"the peace of God that transcends all understanding" (Philippians 4:7). And not fragile freedom, as the world offers, but freedom from the sin that enslaves us all. "If you hold to my teaching, you are really my disciples," Jesus says. "Then you will know the truth and the truth will set you free" (John 8:31-32).

Above all, He offers the ultimate in having it all—everlasting life, not necessarily to those who can afford a $300 seminar, those who can quote the Bible from end to end, those who piously live the "perfect life," but to those who *believe*.

Some say they have too many unanswered questions to believe. We all have unanswered questions. We always will. But faith is the courage to trust God anyway, the willingness to believe in things unseen. "Trust in the Lord with all your heart and lean not on your own understanding," we're told in Proverbs 3:5. Those who refuse to believe until every question is answered will die believing in nothing. Those who accept the free gift of God—Jesus—will inherit life everlasting.

Grace—God's willingness to forgive us even though we don't deserve it—is the catalyst to Christianity. "By grace you have been saved," Paul says in Ephesians 2:8. That's hard to comprehend because we live in an increasingly cynical culture that believes there's no such thing as a free lunch. But to let in the fresh air of faith, pride must be let go.

"There is a certain pride in man that will give and give, but to come and accept is another thing," wrote Oswald Chambers. "We have to realize that we cannot earn or win anything from God; we must either receive it as a gift or do without it. The greatest blessing spiritually is the knowledge that we are destitute; until we get there Our Lord is powerless."[7]

If the unbeliever's challenge is to accept the free gift, the Christian's challenge is to understand the gift and use it as leverage for change. Some of the unhappiest people on earth, a pastor tells me, are Christians who don't tap the power of Christ. One of the most common statements he hears when counseling Christians is "I can't change the way I am," usually uttered by people who live lives full of regret.

Change is the hallmark of Christianity; it's what turned Paul from a Christ-hater to a Christ-lover; it's what turned a party-crazed kid on my college dorm floor into a well-respected pastor.

Christianity consists not of perfect people, but of changing people. To forego "trying to be good enough" is to find the brave new world God intends for us, a world in which we're not coerced by guilt but empowered by Him to become the people He wants us to be.

Certainly we are influenced by our culture. But we are not at the mercy of that culture. We are not victims, but victors—people who can choose to live differently. We are not chained to guilt; God forgives our failings. And yet do we really realize how free we are—or do we stumble on, carrying the burdens we've always had? When our faith is stripped to its core, do we really believe we've been given a free gift, or are we trying to earn our way to heaven as if life were little more than a prize-laden jog-a-thon? Earning our way by being good enough is impossible. Christ's new covenant—His death on the cross—freed us from trying to obtain an unobtainable perfection.

Being granted freedom is meaningless unless we take advantage of that freedom. After slaves in the U.S. were granted freedom in 1862, many chose to remain with their masters as indentured servants. They knew no other way and found security in not changing. So it is with many of us.

Paul struggled with the very thing centuries ago. If we're saved by grace, he wondered, should we keep on living our old way? "By no means!" he said (Romans 6:15).

We serve a new master, a master who has shown love and compassion for us. In return, we can serve Him—not out of obligation, not to get something in return, but because He first loved us. We should serve God because we *want* to serve Him, not because we're spiritual Scouts who must fulfill some sort of badge requirement.

Similarly, our relationships with others need to be the same way: built on a foundation not of compulsion, but of compassion; not of demanding love in return, but of desiring to selflessly serve. "My command is this," said Jesus, "Love each other as I have loved you. Greater love has no one than this, that he lay down his life for his friends" (John 15:12-13).

It is an awesome responsibility, to love others unconditionally; to love our spouses even when we've been hurt; to love our children even when they are rebellious; to love a friend even when our letters trigger no letter in return. At times we will fail—we're fallible human beings—but without having the courage to try, we will *always* fail.

We cannot do it intellectually. "Belief," wrote Chambers, "is not an intellectual act; belief is a moral act whereby I deliberately commit myself . . . I must *will* to believe, and this can never be done without a violent effort on my part to disassociate myself from my old ways of looking at things, and by putting myself right over on to Him."[8]

In the movie *Lost in America*, perhaps the quintessential film of the boomer generation's quest for meaning, a yuppie couple decide to do part of what Chambers advises: they seek to disassociate themselves from their old way of looking at things. Tired of their fast-track, have-it-all lifestyles, they hit the road in a recreational vehicle to find fulfillment—and themselves.

After finding neither, they wind up in New York and, briefcases in hand, resume the very lifestyle from which they had escaped. Though the film's upbeat music suggests a happy ending, what hope is there that the couple will find any more fulfillment in New York than in L.A.? It's the baby boom's lament: same song, different verse. The couple thought that changing their environment and circumstances would magically bring new meaning, that finding fulfillment was some sort of do-it-yourself project. But what needed changing was *them*. And as Chambers suggests, that comes about only through our willingness to trust the true One who created us.

God's path is the only one that leads to the land of contentment. But to walk on that path we must be willing to believe, risk, change. "Do not conform any longer to the pattern of this world, but be transformed by the renewing of your mind," wrote Paul. "Then you will be able to test and approve what God's will is—his good, pleasing and perfect will" (Romans 12:2).

We're not told to escape reality, nor to transform ourselves. We're told to accept the realness of God and allow Him to lead us, change us, renew us. For in Him lies The Secret that so many are hopelessly seeking elsewhere. A secret that involves placing the Creator of the universe above earthly idols, others above ourselves. A secret found not in fantasy, but through faith.

The Choice

It's August in Mendenhall, Miss., where it's so hot that the local newspaper runs what's called a "misery index." High temperatures and high humidity have sent the misery index soaring. And over the years, high rates of poverty and high incidents of racism have sent the state's misery index soaring.

After playing a game of street baseball, I talk to an eight-year-old boy who has nine sisters and five brothers. He lives with his grandmother. His mother lives in a nearby city. "I don't have a daddy yet," he tells me.

Walking downtown, I see an advertisement from a local church extending an invitation to worship Sunday morning. The ad doesn't say so, but even though it's 1987, don't show up if you're black; you're not allowed.

This is a place where a railroad track separates the white part of town from the black part of town, the latter a run-down area labeled The Quarters, so-called because it's where slaves once were housed. The Quarters is a place that echoes heartache from decades of discrimination. It's the kind of place that made a boy named Dolphus Weary fantasize about someday leaving it all behind.

I have come to Mendenhall to explore a mission opportunity for a Seattle-area church. While here, I learn about what became of Dolphus Weary and his fantasy.

He was born the son of a sharecropper in southern Mississippi in 1945. He grew up in a house without running water, plumbing and, not incidentally, a father. He spent his days picking cotton and dreaming about what it was like on the outside.[9]

Weary grew up in a time when black men were occasionally lynched, when three civil rights workers were murdered in Mississippi, when the admission of a black student to the University of Mississippi triggered violent riots.

For Dolphus Weary, Mississippi was hopeless. And so his cotton-field fantasy was a small one: to get out.

The chance came. He graduated valedictorian of his high school class and was voted Most Likely to Succeed. He was offered a basketball scholarship at Los Angeles Baptist College. He and a friend were the first two blacks to graduate from the school.

At the time, Weary felt he had arrived. He had beaten the odds, triumphed over poverty and racism, proven the doubters wrong. His dream was unfolding. Now, he would get married, get a master's degree, settle down in California and live happily ever after, far from Mississippi and its misery index. He would embrace the life he'd been deprived of. For once, Weary could choose to do exactly what he wanted to do.

He chose to return to Mendenhall, Miss. In the movie, *Trip to Bountiful*, an elderly woman feels compelled to return to the town where she had grown up, to remember what it had been like. In real life,

Weary felt compelled to return to the town where he had grown up, to envision what it *could* be like.

And so a man who had beaten all sorts of odds to achieve the cultural equivalent of success gave it all up to return to the poorest county in Mississippi. At first, he wasn't even sure why he had returned; he only knew that he must.

He prayed for leading and prayed some more. And, soon, a dream of revitalizing Mendenhall took shape. Something had to be done to break this cycle of poverty, this specter of racism, this black hole of hopelessness. Somehow, the spiritual and social threads that Christ so perfectly intertwined had to be woven into this place.

Weary began by developing programs for youth that emphasized skills that students needed to get into college. A gymnasium and school were built. A church, farm, thrift store, health center and law clinic were established.

Volunteers from churches around the country trickled into Mendenhall to help, some on a short-term basis; others came and never left. A school teacher from Chicago became the school superintendent. An attorney with a graduate degree from Columbia University gave up her chance for a six-figure income to help establish justice in a small town where there was little. A doctor from New York gave up the good life to bring comfort to Mendenhall's ill—and still found time to play the organ at church on Sunday mornings.

Amazing things were happening. Eighteen-year-old youths destined to wind up working in a local factory for minimum wage started leaving instead for college. Weary was being asked to speak at churches around the country about how programs similar to Mendenhall Ministries could be established in other places. The icy chasm between blacks and whites in Mendenhall began slowly melting; in 1989, members of the First Baptist Church in the white community held a joint Easter celebration with the predominantly black Mendenhall Bible Church.

For Weary and those who joined his cause, the gospel had become not just a Sunday-morning add-on to their lives, but the thread that ran through every part of their lives. Not just a reason to establish "programs," but a way to heal the physical and spiritual lives of people. Not a free pass to "success" but an empowering force of compassion.

Rags-to-riches stories usually end with someone owning a Fortune 500 company or being elected governor or driving a Mercedes. This one does not. For true riches are measured not in dollars, but in devotion—to God and to people.

On my last day in Mendenhall, Weary drove me to the local hospital in his battered station wagon to proudly show me and some others his newborn son—a son who will grow up in a better world because his father chose to help ease the misery index rather than flee from it, chose to give instead of receive, chose faith in God instead of the fantasy of man.

The Centerpiece

ह

It was the Christmas when I heard all the carols but never listened to the words, the Christmas when I was burdened with more questions than buoyed with answers.

Like nearly everyone else, I had spent the past few weeks going through the motions, the holiday equivalent of teeth brushing. Not something you did because you were compelled to do so, but because it was part of life's routine.

I had done the expected: Buying presents. Singing songs. And looking at the residential light displays, including the manger scene with the shepherds gathered around the Christ child while Santa watched approvingly from the roof of the manger.

Now it was Christmas Day, the cymbal clash at the end of the drum roll.

But where was the magic?

Certainly not in the weather. Like most Christmases in Oregon, it was one of those in-between days—too cold to be pleasant, too warm to snow. It was one of those drab days you wanted the weather to do something—suddenly muster itself into a driving rainstorm or break into soul-cleansing sunshine. *Anything.* But it would not.

As we made our way north to my uncle's house, the clouds hung low over the Coast Range and, like my own overcast mood, showed no signs of clearing. White Christmases, I had decided, were reserved for schmaltzy Christmas movies and Kodak commercials in which everybody was so busy smiling and hugging and spreading holiday cheer that they didn't stop to consider what the celebration was all about.

Two thousand years ago, the Wise Men had seen a star in the sky—a message of the messiah, of healing, of hope. As we drove along, it all seemed so far away; not two thousand years away, but light years away. I looked at the houses as we drove by, imagining families eating dinner and opening presents and watching football on TV.

But where was the message?

Certainly not in our 20th-century celebrations. On this day, the sign in the sky was not a star, but the smokestack of a paper plant. We always drove by the paper plant en route to my uncle's house, and Christmas Day was the lone day of the year when it didn't operate. That was our sign, our reminder that a child had been born. Rejoice! For unto freeway passengers was given a day without the stench of smoke.

We arrived at my uncle's house, four more people in a mix of diversity, linked not by common interests or values, but by blood. There had been a time when I had felt keenly part of this clan, as if returning each year were like putting on a pair of well-worn tennis shoes that fit just right.

This year, I felt no such comfort. Perhaps it was my age. In my late teens, I was too old to believe in the magic of Santa Claus, too young to believe in children's laughter, too collegiate to be engrossed in the Christmas story, too confused to be anything other than a cynic in holiday disguise.

This was my year of questioning, the year I wanted to quit college, stop writing and become a milk man; the year my faith had been battered by so many professors and live-for-today dorm neighbors that I had almost come to believe it was easier to switch than fight.

Where was the meaning?

Certainly not in this living room of people, I thought as I half-listened to the small talk. They were good folks. But it was all so programmed. The same people. The same house. The same conversations. The same guitar-only Christmas music coming softly from the stereo.

It was all warm and comfortable and cozy—we seemingly had it all—and yet it left me empty, as if something were missing. We ate the same kind of food we ate every year and made all the too-full jokes about how much we'd overeaten.

Then it happened. As we readied to open our presents—the last stop on this train ride of tradition—my uncle stood up in front of us and said he had something he wanted to share with us. People looked puzzled. This was not part of the routine. This was not written in the script.

My uncle looked around the room. He said he had been thinking, and decided it was important to remember why we celebrate Christmas. He wanted to read something to help remind us. I figured he would read us the Christmas story—that's a safe thing to read at Christmas—but he did not. Instead, he read us a piece written by an anonymous author, a piece called "One Solitary Life":

> *Here is a man*
> *who was born of Jewish parents*
> *the child of a peasant woman . . .*
> *He never wrote a book*
> *He never held an office.*
> *He never owned a home.*
> *He never had a family.*
> *He never went to college.*
> *He never put foot*
> *inside a big city.*
> *He never travelled two hundred*
> *miles from the place*
> *where he was born.*
> *He never did one of the things*
> *that usually accompany greatness.*
> *He had no credentials but himself . . .*

The two dozen people in the living room were still. Nobody even whispered. We all just looked at my uncle as he continued, realizing that we were in the midst of something strangely special.

> *While still a young man,*
> *the tide of popular opinion*
> *turned against him.*
> *His friends ran away.*
> *One of them denied him. . . .*
> *He was nailed to a cross*
> *between two thieves.*
> *His executioners gambled for*

the only piece of property
he had on earth . . . his coat.
When he was dead
he was taken down
and laid in a borrowed grave
through the pity of a friend.

My uncle's eyes grew misty. So did some others. So did mine.

Nineteen wide centuries
have come and gone
and he is the centerpiece
of the human race and the
leader of the column of progress.
I am far within the mark
when I say that all the armies
that ever marched,
and all the navies
that were ever built . . .
have not affected the life of man
upon earth
as powerfully as has that
One Solitary Life.

Had this been the movies, a light snow would have begun to fall outside. But snow did not fall. Nor did a star appear in the sky. Instead, my uncle simply sat down. Slowly, people began making small talk again before opening presents.

I don't know how the reading affected others. I only know that for me, it was more than a temporary cease-fire for my inner turmoil. It was light for my darkness of doubt. It was reassurance that the child of that peasant woman had grown into human-kind's only hope. It was a reminder that, amid the routine, what had been missing on this Christmas Day was not snow on the ground or a star in the sky.

What had been missing—both on this day and in my life—was the guest of honor, the centerpiece of the celebration.

NOTES

Understanding the Cultural Forces
1. Nancy Gibbs, "How America Has Run Out of Time," *Time*, April 24, 1989, p. 58.
2. "U.S. Teen-agers Unhealthy, Panel Says," *The Register-Guard* (Eugene, OR), June 9, 1990, p. 3A.
3. Martin E.P. Seligman, "Boomer Blues," *Psychology Today*, October 1988, pp. 50-55.
4. Paula Rinehart, "The Pivotal Generation: Who Will Tap the Latent Idealism of the Baby Boomers?" *Christianity Today*, Oct. 6, 1989, p. 21.
5. Tom Morganthau, "Decade Shock," *Newsweek*, Sept. 5, 1988, p. 14.
6. James Webb, "A Legacy for My Daughter," *Newsweek*, Nov. 7, 1988, p. 13.
7. Landon Y. Jones, *Great Expectations: America & the Baby Boom Generation* (New York: Coward, McCann & Geoghegan, 1980), p. 1.

Chapter 1: Trading Consumerism for Contentment
1. Lewis H. Lapham, Michael Pollan and Eric Etheridge, *The Harper's Index Book* (New York: Henry Holt and Co., 1987), p. 20.
2. Ibid., p. 26.
3. Ibid.

Chapter 2: Trading Fast Forward for Play and Pause
1. The Associated Press, "News Crew Was Beaten, Interrogated," *The Register-Guard* (Eugene, OR), March 4, 1991, p. 5A.
2. "Piece Meal Dinners," *U.S. News & World Report*, April 23, 1990, p. 78.
3. Tom Peters and Nancy Austin, *A Passion for Excellence* (New York: Random House, 1985), p. 419.
4. Ralph Brauer, "Learning from Millie," *Newsweek*, Nov. 20, 1989, p. 10.
5. Landon Y. Jones, *Great Expectations: America & the Baby Boom Generation* (New York: Coward, McCann & Geoghegan, 1980), p. 1.

Chapter 3: Trading Trends for Tradition
1. Janice Castro, "The Simple Life," *Time*, April 8, 1991, pp. 58-64.
2. Natalie de Combray, "Volunteering in America," *American Demographics*, March 1987, p. 50-52.
3. Bob Welch, "From the Mouths of Babes Comes a Cry for Help," *The Journal-American* (Bellevue, WA), Aug. 15, 1988, p. A3.
4. William A. Donohue, *The New Freedom* (New Brunswick, NJ: Transaction Press, 1990), p. 100.

Chapter 4: Trading Technology for Talk
1. Blayne Cutler, "Meet Jane Doe," *American Demographics*, June 1989, p. 24.
2. William A. Donohue, *The New Freedom*, (New Brunswick, NJ: Transaction Pub., 1990), p. 20.
3. Blayne Cutler, "Where Does the Free Time Go?" *American Demographics*, November 1990, p. 38.

4. Thornton Wilder, *Our Town* (New York: Coward-McCann, Inc., 1939), p. 83.

Chapter 5: Trading Self-Centeredness for Self-Sacrifice
1. Landon Y. Jones, *Great Expectations: America & the Baby Boom Generation* (New York: Coward, McCann & Geoghegan, 1980), p. 260.
2. Oswald Chambers, *My Utmost for His Highest* (Westwood, NJ: Barbour and Company, Inc., 1963), p. 204.

Chapter 6: Trading Style for Substance
1. The Associated Press, "Milli Vanilli? Just a Symptom of 'Reality Erosion,'" *The Register-Guard* (Eugene, OR), Dec. 2, 1990, p. 4B.
2. Bob Welch, "Image and the '80s," *Focus on the Family*, January 1988, p. 7.
3. Jerry Manker, *Four Arguments for the Elimination of Television* (New York: Quill, 1978), p. 255.

Chapter 7: Trading Promises for Perseverance
1. "When Family Will Have a New Definition," *U.S. News & World Report*, May 9, 1983, p. 94.
2. Lewis H. Lapham, Michael Polland and Eric Etheridge, *The Harper's Index Book* (New York: Henry Holt & Co., 1987), p. 53.
3. "What Happened to the Family?," *Newsweek Special Issue*, Winter/Spring 1990, pp. 16-20.
4. Landon Y. Jones, *Great Expectations: America & the Baby Boom Generation* (New York: Coward, McCann & Geoghegan, 1980), p. 187.
5. William A. Donohue, *The New Freedom* (New Brunswick, NJ: Transaction Press, 1990), p. 75.
6. Cheryl Russell, *One Hundred Predictions for the Baby Boom, The Next Fifty Years* (New York: Plenum Press, 1987), p. 107.
7. Anastasia Toufexis, "The Lasting Wounds of Divorce," *Time*, Feb. 6, 1989, p. 61.

Chapter 8: Trading Compromise for Commitment
1. T. Berry Brazelton, "Why Is America Failing Its Children?" *New York Times Magazine*, Sept. 9, 1990, p. 50.
2. "Offbeat News Stories of 1988," *The World Almanac* (New York: Pharos Books, 1989), p. 927.
3. Anastasia Toufexis, "Struggling for Sanity," *Time*, Oct. 8, 1990, p. 47.
4. Ibid.
5. Cheryl Russell, "What's Your Hurry?" *American Demographics*, April 1989, p. 2.
6. Landon Y. Jones, *Great Expectations: America & the Baby Boom Generation* (New York: Coward, McCann & Geoghegan, 1980), p. 216.
7. David Gelman, "A Much Riskier Passage," *Newsweek Special Issue*, Winter/Spring 1990, p. 10.
8. Jill Smolowe, "To Grandma's House We Go," *Time*, Nov. 5, 1990, p. 86.
9. Sara Davidson, "Kids in the Fast Lane," *The New York Times Magazine*, Oct. 16, 1988, p. 52.

10. Ross Campbell, *How to Really Love Your Child* (Wheaton, IL: Victor Books, 1980), p. 56.
11. K. Zinsmeister, "Hard Truths About Day Care," *Reader's Digest*, October 1988, pp. 88-93.
12. "The New Necessities," *Christianity Today*, April 21, 1989, p. 13.
13. Philip Elmer-Dewitt, "The Great Experiment," *Time*, Fall 1990, p. 75.

Chapter 9: Trading Rights for Responsibilities
1. Roger Rosenblatt, "The Freedom of the Damned," *Time*, Oct. 6, 1986, p. 98.
2. John Russo, " 'Reel' Vs. Real Violence," *Newsweek*, Feb. 19, 1990, p. 10.
3. New York Times Wire Service, "Studies Find Individualism Is Rare," *The Register-Guard* (Eugene, OR), Dec. 25, 1990, p. 7A.
4. Melinda Blau, *American Health Magazine*, reprinted in *Utne Reader*, November/December 1990, p. 61.
5. Melissa Ludtke, "A Letter From the Publisher," *Time*, Aug. 8, 1988, p. 4.
6. The Associated Press, "U.S. Leads World in Imprisonment, Report Says," *The Register-Guard* (Eugene, OR), Jan. 5, 1991, p. 9A.
7. Rosenblatt, "Freedom of the Damned," p. 98.

Chapter 10: Trading Fantasy for Faith
1. Rebecca Piirto, "Looking to Connect Again," *American Demographics*, Aug. 1989, p. 38.
2. Landon Y. Jones, *Great Expectations: America & the Baby Boom Generation* (New York: Coward, McCann & Geoghegan, 1980), p. 123.
3. Martin E.P. Seligman, "Boomer Blues," *Psychology Today*, October 1988, pp. 50-55.
4. Cheryl Russell, "Everyone's Gone to the Moon," *American Demographics*, Feb. 1990, p. 2.
5. Charles Leerhsen, "Unite and Conquer," *Newsweek*, Feb. 5, 1990, p. 50.
6. Kenneth Woodward, "A Time to Seek," *Newsweek*, Dec. 17, 1990, p. 56.
7. Oswald Chambers, *My Utmost for His Highest* (Westwood, NJ: Barbour and Co., Inc., 1963), p. 247.
8. Ibid., pp. 265-266.
9. Some information from this chapter comes from Dolphus Weary, *I Ain't Comin' Back* (Wheaton, IL: Tyndale House, 1990). Used by permission.